DIECAST RAILWAYS TOY FIGURES TINPLATE T

CW00666176

» Publisher
Rob McDonnell 01778 391181
robm@warnersgroup.co.uk

» Editor
Rob Burman 01778 392400
robb@warnersgroup.co.uk

» Group Key Account Manager
Claire Morris 01778 391179
clairem@warnersgroup.co.uk

» Head of Design & Production
Lynn Wright 01778 391139
lynnw@warnersgroup.co.uk

» Editorial Design Cathy Herron

» Advertising Production
Kate Michelson 01778 392420
katem@warnersgroup.co.uk

» Marketing Manager
Sarah Stephens 01778 395007
sarahs@warnersgroup.co.uk

Toy Collectors Price Guide 2016 is published annually by Warners Group Publications Plc, The Maltings, West Street, Bourne, Lincolnshire PE10 9PH, England.

» Newstrade Distribution
This magazine is distributed by:
Warners Group Publications Ltd
Tel: 01778 391150

WARNERS | This publication is printed by Warners 01778 395111

Welcome

A s usual, it gives me great pleasure to welcome you, dear reader, to our latest annual *Toy Collectors Price Guide*, which gives you an estimate on how much your vintage toy collection might be worth. We've scoured auction house results from around the country (and even the world in some cases) to bring you a super selection of collectables, along with detailed descriptions and large, full colour photographs. Whether you collect diecast vehicles, model locomotives, toy figures, TV and film memorabilia, tinplate or something a little more unusual, I'm sure you'll find plenty to tickle your fancy in this year's guide. In the pages ahead you'll find a whopping 1,129 listings with a staggering total of £175,953... and that doesn't include our expanded eBuys section.

As for the toy collecting market, well it certainly doesn't seem to be slowing down with some genres positively booming throughout 2015. What's more, the interest in the mainstream media continues apace with articles or TV shows regularly extolling the virtues (and potential profits) in toy collecting. Meanwhile, toy fairs and auctions continue to attract the buyers and sellers, eager to add to their collections or perhaps move some unwanted items on to others.

Here at the *Toy Collectors Price Guide*, we've also continued to make some changes to the content based on your feedback. Some asked for longer features to read,

in order to break up the results, so we've included a few favourites from the pages of the *Collectors Gazette*, which I'm sure you'll enjoy. Elsewhere we've increased the number of listings in our eBuys section to include even more items. Online auctions are becoming an increasingly important part of toy collecting, with some amazing results, so it makes sense to include a selection

of the millions of toys sold on the website throughout the year.

Well, all that remains is for me to say that we all hope you enjoy this year's edition and that 2016 continues to be a bumper year for toy collecting. Happy collecting everyone!

Rob Burman
Editor

Rob

CONTACT: Toy Collectors Price Guide, Warners Group Publications, West Street, Bourne, Lincs PE10 9PH.
Tel: **01778 392400** Fax: **01778 392422**.

Guide to...
Buying at Auction

Choosing to buy your collectables at auction doesn't have to be a daunting task, just read our beginner's guide below to help get you started.

Throughout the course of this publication, you'll see hundreds of auction results for a vast amount of different toys. However, for someone who has never been to an auction, the very thought can be a little off putting. All those comedy sketches of people sneezing during an auction and then buying a vase for £100,000 probably don't help either. However, the truth is that toy auctions tend to be a far more relaxed affair with many people heading along for a bit of a chinwag with fellow collectors, as well as potentially bidding on some vintage collectables. In fact, the opportunity to meet others – particularly during the preview day – is a great reason to visit an auctioneer because it will potentially help to expand your collecting knowledge.

The preview day (or morning in the case of some auctioneers) is certainly a great place to start if you're planning on bidding for the first time. This is because you'll get to look at any items you want to buy, rather than just relying on a description in the auction catalogue. Some auctioneers will also be happy to let you test an item to check it's working... just make sure you ask someone first before whizzing a locomotive around an imaginary piece of track. What's more, the auctioneer or expert will often be on-hand during the preview day, giving you the chance to ask any more questions about the condition of the toy you're thinking of purchasing.

Something else to do before the auction is register your details with the auctioneer. Rather than the aforementioned comedy

Now you can visit an auction yourself or bid online, thanks to numerous websites.

sketch, most auctioneers require you to hold up a number once you've finished bidding, which corresponds to your details... so this should make accidental purchases very tricky! Once you have your number, the auctioneer will be able to keep track of everything you've bought, so when you're ready to leave, you'll be able to show them that and they'll tally up how much you owe (assuming you've got enough cash with you).

Finally on the preparation front, make sure you do your research before you starting bidding because there's nothing worse than getting something home and realising it wasn't what you were after. If you can't make it to the preview day, then ring the auctioneer to ask questions. If you're on the internet, you can even ask the saleroom to send over more pictures for you to peruse at your leisure. Research is key to finding a good buy!

So, you've done your research, you've seen the toys and you've got your number... it's time to start bidding. The key here is not

to get carried away because some will get caught up in the moment. If you've done your research then, hopefully, you'll know what a decent price is for the piece you're interested in. Before the auction, consider how much you're willing to pay and stick to that because once you start going over a set amount then it might be a slippery slope. Also, don't show your hand too early to others in the room and don't seem overly eager. Typically the auctioneer will start at a price and, if there's no interest, the starting price will drop – don't think you have to start bidding straight away. Also, when you're working out your set amount bear in mind that auctioneers add buyer's commission, as well as taking a commission from the seller too. Normally buyer's commission tends to be around 20%, so that will be added to whatever amount the hammer falls on, e.g. you may 'win' the lot for £500 but the final invoice will be around £600.

If you can't make it to the auction on the day, then consider leaving a bid on the books or

asking to make a telephone bid. The former is a great way to ensure you don't spend too much, as you can leave your bid with the auction house, safe in the knowledge that you're not going to get carried away.

Of course, an increasingly popular way to bid is online, using websites like The Saleroom or the auctioneer's own website, which means you can sit at home drinking a cuppa while bidding on your lots. Something to bear in mind, however, and something that we've seen can be frustrating for auctioneers is when online bidders leave it until the last moment to bid, a bit like they would on eBay. So, the auctioneer will be about to sell the lot when suddenly a last minute online bid comes in. Unlike eBay this isn't a guarantee that you'll win. Also consider that if you've never bid online before, then it could take some time to register all your details on the site, which you're required to do before you can bid. Don't miss out on the item you want because you're still filling in an address form! ∎

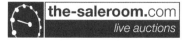

Guide to...
Future
collectables

Take a look into the *Toy Collectors Price Guide* crystal ball to see what could be making big money at auction in the years to come.

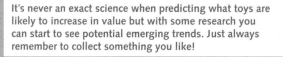
It's never an exact science when predicting what toys are likely to increase in value but with some research you can start to see potential emerging trends. Just always remember to collect something you like!

Each year in the *Toy Collectors Price Guide* we look at the current trends to see if there are any toys flying under the radar that could become 'collectables of the future'. These items are toys that occasionally appear at auction (or more often on websites like eBay) but potentially haven't reached their peak price. It's a bit like someone buying *Star Wars* figures in the 1980s because they thought they might increase in value... and boy, what a good bet that would have been! Of course, predicting these collectables of the future can be down to luck but if you keep a close eye on buying trends at auction and regularly look at the sold items on eBay, then you can start to see patterns.

Obviously there's no guarantee that they will increase in value and our advice to someone is always to collect something that you're going to enjoy collecting, rather than only buying it because you think it's going to be worth a fortune. That way if it doesn't increase, then at least you've got something nice to keep! So, with that caveat in mind, let's gaze once more into the *Toy Collectors Price Guide* crystal ball...

GHOSTBUSTERS
2016 is a key year for *Ghostbusters* because there's going to be a new film featuring an all-new female cast of spook hunters. Although the original film was released in 1984 it has remained in the zeitgeist to this day with a sequel in 1989, rumours of a third film since the 1990s, videogames, cartoons and comics. *The Real Ghostbusters*, a cartoon that started in 1986, provided children with plenty of toys based on Peter

Venkman, Ray Stantz and the rest of the crew. Produced by Kenner, the action figures, vehicles and ghosts are becoming more valuable and with the film due next year, interest could increase.

X-WING MINIATURES GAME
You would think that almost every *Star Wars* toy imaginable would now instantly be considered as collectable, however there's one *Star Wars* product that might not fit into the traditional toy category and is therefore passing some people by. In 2013 Fantasy Flight Games released the X-Wing Miniatures Game, a tabletop wargame that involves tiny painted spaceships from the *Star Wars* franchise. The ships come in blister packs and, because players want to use them as part of their fleet, they're eagerly ripped open and immediately placed on the tabletop ready for action. As a result, there's a chance that if the game goes out of production not many collectors will have the ships in mint condition. What's

more, the prices aren't bad too, with some ships starting around the £10 mark.

LEGO IDEAS
Admittedly, LEGO regularly features in our Collectables of the Future section but, then again, we continue to see some astounding prices for certain LEGO kits and even the Minifigures can be worth hundreds. If you're interested in starting a LEGO collection, then perhaps consider the LEGO Ideas range, previously known as LEGO Cuusoo. The Ideas kits are actually based on designs created by the LEGO community and if they get 10,000 votes on the Ideas website, then LEGO potentially releases them as an official set. So far LEGO has released Ideas sets based on famous films like *Ghostbusters* and *Back to the Future*, along with original themes like a group of female scientists and a futuristic robot suit. Only a few Ideas kits come out every year, so starting a new collection won't be overwhelming

and because they tend to have lower print runs than standard sets, there's the potential for them to become more valuable.

JURASSIC PARK
Earlier this year *Jurassic World*, the latest film in the blockbuster *Jurassic Park* series, became one of the most successful movies in history making more than $1 billion at the box office. As a result there's been a surge of interest in original *Jurassic Park* toys produced by Kenner in the early 1990s. In particular iconic dinosaurs like the T-rex with electronic roar are starting to make serious money on eBay and regularly sell for more than £100. What's more, it's been confirmed that *Jurassic World* is the first in a new series of films, so this spike in popularity is likely to continue for some time. Also consider picking up the recently released *Jurassic World* LEGO sets, as they combine two popular themes so will appeal to more potential toy collectors. ■

SELLING YOUR TOYS & MODELS?

Warwick and Warwick have an expanding requirement for toys and model collections, British and worldwide and for diecast models, trains/train sets, model soldiers and toys of individual value. Our customer base is increasing dramatically and we need an ever larger supply of quality material to keep pace with demand. The market has never been stronger and if you are considering the sale of your collection, now is the time to act.

FREE VALUATIONS

We will provide a free, professional and without obligation valuation of your collection. Either we will make you a fair, binding private treaty offer, or we will recommend inclusion of your property in our next specialist public auction.

FREE TRANSPORTATION

We can arrange insured transportation of your collection to our Warwick offices completely free of charge. If you decline our offer, we ask you to cover the return carriage costs only.

FREE VISITS

Visits by our valuers are possible anywhere in the country or abroad, usually within 48 hours, in order to value larger collections. Please telephone for details.

ADVISORY DAYS

We are staging a series of advisory days across the country. Please visit our website or telephone for further details.

EXCELLENT PRICES

Because of the strength of our customer base we are in a position to offer prices that we feel sure will exceed your expectations.

ACT NOW

Telephone or email Richard Beale today with details of your property.

DIECAST	RAILWAYS	TOY FIGURES	TINPLATE	TV & FILM	OTHERS	EBUYS

Introduction to...
Collecting
Diecast

Typically diecast collecting continues to be one of the most established areas of vintage toy collecting, with the diecast section forming the foundations of a sale. As such it's our biggest category.

Well, as per usual, diecast has continued to be one of the main factors in toy sales around the country, with some stand out collections coming under the hammer over the past year. Diecast models – whether they be from Corgi, Dinky, Matchbox or one of the other many makers – are really the bread of butter of a toy auction and more often than not form the core for an auctioneer, along with model railways.

Something that's been apparent since the last *Toy Collectors Price Guide* is that quality continues to be a huge factor in price and can really make a massive difference when the hammer goes down. We've come across numerous traders and auctioneers saying time and time again that "quality sells" and collectors are willing to pay the big money for examples in superb condition. Often the difference between a decent diecast model and a top notch one can run into the hundreds.

Again, this goes down to the fact that diecast collecting is easily one of the most established genres of vintage toy collecting, with numerous guides charting the variations available and the potential valuations of each piece. Head to an auction or a swapmeet

and you'll often see punters clutching a copy of their favourite guide to make sure they're getting a good deal. Of course, those top prices quoted in those guides are for the mint examples, so that's certainly worth bearing in mind when you're totting up a potential valuation for your collection.

In terms of diecast brands, then we've heard that Corgi is performing slightly better in terms of prices than its rival Dinky and there are a number of theories as to why that might be. One collector explained that it could be down to something simple, like the fact Corgi models are often much brighter and display better. While another collector explained that because

Dinky models have been around for longer it means that those who remember playing with them as children are now selling their collections, rather than purchasing more. It'll be interesting to see if that trend continues in the months to come.

If you're just starting out with your diecast collection and have picked up this annual as an introduction, then the key thing to pay attention to when considering a purchase at auction is the auctioneer's description because it'll contain vital information, such as whether the colour is a rare version, if the box is complete and if the model is a pre-production example. The latter is an interesting area of

diecast collecting that appears to be growing, as die-hard collectors are keen to get their hands on unusual pieces that didn't make it into general circulation. This is particularly true of Matchbox models and the factory appears to have often produced numerous colour trials of models that somehow made their way off the production line and into the hands of eager collectors. Something we often say here in these introductions is that it pays to do your homework and, when it comes to pre-production samples, that's certainly true as these can be highly sought after. Hopefully across these pages you'll see some of those unusual pieces and others you remember owning! ∎

327 We've actually increased the amount of diecast listings compared to last year!

60 2016 is going to be a key year for diecast fans, as Corgi is celebrating its 60th anniversary.

£159 A rough estimate shows the average price paid was £159.

£1,600 This was the hammer price for a Dinky No. 153 Standard Vanguard Saloon.

£52,003 Here's the total amount raised by diecast sales listed in this edition.

On the buses

Celebrating the 60th anniversary of the iconic AEC Routemaster bus with Corgi Toys.

ABOVE With a chocolate bar called Double Decker, Cadbury's couldn't resist releasing a promotional version of the Routemaster, as made by Corgi in 1977.

Just like cups of tea, the Queen, Big Ben and red telephone boxes, there is one thing that typifies good old Blighty... particularly to our friends over in America. The bright red AEC Routemaster double decker bus has become a staple image of Great Britain with numerous appearances in TV shows and films since it was first introduced in 1954 - it was even turned into a cartoon character called Topper Deckington III in Disney's Cars 2. So, as the red wonder celebrates 60 years, let's take a brief glimpse at the bus' history and the numerous Corgi replicas inspired by it.

The Routemaster was created in a partnership between London Transport, Associated Equipment Company (AEC) and Park Royal Vehicles. Work began on designing the Routemaster in 1947, with the objective being to design a bus that was lighter to make it more fuel efficient, easier to operate and could be maintained at the existing Aldenham Works.

In 1954 the design team delivered the first prototype – a vehicle capable of carrying 64 passengers (previous buses only carried 56) with a half-cab, front-mounted engine and open rear platform. One of the most pioneering aspects of the design was that open rear platform, which allowed passengers to jump on and off the bus, rather than having to wait to board or alight at an official stop. Of course, a conductor was required to make sure no one got a free ride but, again, this help to cut down boarding times to make the

journeys more efficient because he could collect fares without requiring the bus to stop. The Routemaster was first exhibited at the Earls Court Commercial Motor Show in 1954 and the first four prototypes were placed into service between 1956 and '58.

Routemasters continued to be something of a success for 25 years before they started to be withdrawn in the 1970s when the desire was for single man operations to cut down on costs. By the 1980s the number of Routemasters in the fleet dropped dramatically but the final nail in the coffin came in March 2003 when Transport for London managing director Peter Hendy said that for TfL to become compliant with the Disability Discrimination Act it needed to ensure all its fleet were low-floor double deckers or articulated buses. As a result the last Routemasters were withdrawn from general service in December 2005. Thankfully though, many of the old Routemasters were snapped up by private charter companies and one continues to be used on a heritage route, ensuring that even after 60 years this great British icon can still be seen on the nation's roads.

CORGI ROUTEMASTERS
One of the most prevalent manufacturers of Routemaster replicas has to be Corgi and between 1964 and 1986 it produced more than 60 Routemasters (you

The Routemaster has become one of the iconic vehicles that's used to represent 'England' in countless films and television series.

wait for one bus to come along... and then 60 come at once) in a range of liveries. There are two distinct periods for these models, the first from 1964 until 1975 and the second from 1975 onwards, with clear differences between the two periods.

The first casting saw Corgi only produce a closed top version and all were listed as model number 468. Measuring 114mm, the first issue Routemaster has a diecast body made from two separate castings that make up the lower and upper decks, which are separated by a white plastic joint. The baseplate is diecast, painted grey and stamped 'Corgi

Toys', 'LONDON TRANSPORT', 'ROUTEMASTER', 'MADE IN ENGLAND' and also has the patent number '904525'. Early issues have turned metal wheels with rubber tyres but from 1973 these were replaced by cast metal wheels with plastic tyres, then in 1974/75 Whizzwheels also made an appearance.

Earlier issues also feature jewelled headlights but these were replaced by cast-in painted lights in 1973. Decals are transfer prints and there is only a board at the front. Other details to look out for include spring suspension, windows, a metal platform handrail and figures of a driver

A great illustration of how Corgi re-used the first edition Routemaster casting but just added new adverts for different releases. This is the Outspan Oranges example from Australia.

The Red Rose Tea piece from Canada, another attractive bus that's become very collectable for Corgi collectors and bus enthusiasts alike.

Madame Tussaud's from good old Blighty. No doubt this was a popular pick-up for tourists to the famous London attraction.

ABOVE Here you can get a closer look at the Great Book of Corgi bus. It has a rather attractive cream and pale blue finish... a nice contrast to the typical bright red of the London buses.

ABOVE The Routemaster was the star of the show in this charming London Transport Gift Set, first released in 1971. The set includes a great display with iconic London buildings in the background, along with a (hopefully not to scale) model of a typical British Bobby. *Images courtesy of Vectis.*

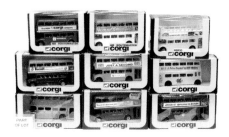

and conductor. Interior seats are either white or cream.

For the second casting, Corgi increased the size a little and the model now measured 123mm, plus it also began making open top examples. Again the body is made from two separate castings, making the lower and upper decks, but this time the decks are separated by a cream plastic joint or a coloured plastic joint for the numerous special editions. Meanwhile on the base the buses were stamped with: 'CORGI', 'LONDON TRANSPORT', 'ROUTEMASTER' and 'MADE IN ENGLAND' until 1983 when 'LONDON TRANSPORT' and

'ROUTEMASTER' were both removed.

For the later issues, the original transfer logos were replaced by stick on labels, which in turn were superseded by tampo printing in the 1980s. Once again the seats tended to be white or cream but some of the specials feature different colours to match the colourful paint finish, like the orange interior for the C470 Disneyland model. Early issues of the second casting did include conductors and drivers (like C469 BTA Welcome to Britain) but later entries into the range did away with the figures. As for the wheels all of the second castings

have Whizzwheels with either chrome or painted wheel hubs.

NEW CORGI ROUTEMASTERS

However, Corgi hasn't stopped producing new Routemaster replicas and this year announced it would be producing two brand new 1/50 scale buses to celebrate the bus' 60 year milestone. These new models include Route 11 'Liverpool Street Station' and RM 8 First in Operation – sadly the second one is going to miss the 60th anniversary, after being pushed back to 2015 but Liverpool Street is still on track for a September release. ∎

ABOVE LEFT
Here's an example of all the different Routemaster buses produced by Corgi. They're available in all manner of different colours and liveries covering numerous different companies.

ABOVE CENTRE
Yet more Routemasters from Corgi!

ABOVE RIGHT
Marcel van Cleemput, ex Corgi toy designer known as 'Mr Corgi', released this book in 1989, which included a special edition Routemaster as a great free gift.

Over for Rover

Looking back at the toys inspired by this famous British marque.

The earliest diecast Rover is Dinky's No. 36d Streamlined Saloon.

Around 10 years ago the factory doors closed on one of Britian's famous car manufacturers, ending more than 100 years Rover cars. Throughout that time, particularly in the 1950s and '60s, it made some of Britain's best-loved cars with the introduction of vehicles like the Land Rover. Rover also provided the inspiration for numerous toy cars from Spot-On, Matchbox, Corgi and Dinky. So, let's celebrate this great British marque by looking at some of the diecast vehicles inspired by it.

First a little history about the company because its origins are rather surprising and the first 'Rover' ever produced was actually a tricycle, not a car. The company, initially known as Starley & Sutton Co., was founded in Coventry in 1883 by John Kemp Starley and William Sutton and created the Rover Safety Bicycle, which had two similar-sized wheels, rather than the frankly lethal design of the Penny Farthing. The success of the bicycle led to the company changing its name to the Rover Cycle Company Ltd. in the late 1890s.

From bicycles, Rover then moved to motorbikes and in 1902 produced the Rover Imperial, a 3.5hp diamond-framed motorcycle that sold more than 1,000 units in 1904 – the same year as Starley died. The next big step for Rover came in 1907 when it produced its first automobile: the two-seater Rover Eight. Despite a troubled time in the 1920s, things progressed quite nicely for Rover until the late '60s when it was acquired by the Leyland Motor Corporation, which owned Triumph. In 1968, Leyland merged with British Motor Holdings to become the British Leyland Motor Corporation but Rover struggled throughout the '70s as the British motor industry suffered numerous industrial problems and set-backs.

As a result the '80s and '90s featured numerous mergers and takeovers from the likes of British Aerospace (BAe), then BMW who only kept MINI production while Ford took over Land Rover and in 2000 former Rover executive John Towers created MG Rover. The latter lasted five years and in 2005 was declared insolvent. The MG Rover name was bought by Chinese company Nanjing Automobile, who moved production to China.

DINKY TOYS NO. 36D ROVER STEAMLINED SALOON

One of the earliest Rover models is the Dinky Toys No. 36d Streamlined Saloon with driver and footman, released in 1937. It was also re-released in 1947 without the extra figures. The model resembles the Rover Speed 14, which was launched as a medium-sized four-door family car in 1933 and was given a more streamlined appearance in the late '30s – in the style of the Dinky version.

LAND ROVER

Rover fans had to wait a few years for Dinky's next release, with the No. 27d Land Rover being launched in 1950 – three years after the vehicle was first conceived by Rover. Not only did the versatile off-road vehicle become Rover's most successful product, it also inspired countless models. Among the first was Dinky's Land Rover,

later renumbered to No. 340 in 1954, which was initially sold in trade boxes of four models. It was available in numerous different colours, including dark blue, orange, green and brown. After the renumbering to 340, the Land Rover was sold in individual boxes and came with a plastic, rather than diecast driver.

Following Dinky's take on the Land Rover, rival British diecast company Morestone also threw its hat into the ring with a selection of Land Rover models in the late 1950s. The first, released in 1955, was a larger-scale AA Land Rover measuring 108mm and finished in yellow/black with 'AA Road Service' cast onto the side. It was followed in 1957 by a smaller version of the same model, then Military Police and Breakdown Service versions in 1958.

However, it was really Corgi Toys that took the Land Rover to heart and produced numerous versions throughout the '50s and '60s. Starting with No. 406 Land Rover in 1957, which was finished in yellow or metallic blue, Corgi went on to produce some of the more weird and wonderful

Wonder if modern Corgi would revisit this design for the upcoming General Election?

One of the more unusual Rovers, is this Chipperfields Circus Land Rover Parade Vehicle.

A sporty little number was the Corgi Toys No. 322 Rover 2000 in International

BELOW
A trade pack of Dinky Land Rovers.

ABOVE
More than 35,000 Rover 90s were produced between 1953 and 1959, however according to the Great Book of Corgi, 110,000 models were produced of the same car.

takes on the all-purpose vehicle. Perhaps the most unlikely use is No. 487 Chipperfields Circus Land Rover Parade Vehicle (1965-69), which features a clown and monkey riding in the rear. This brightly-coloured attractive vehicle was based on the Land Rover Public Address Vehicle, released to coincide with the 1964 General Election.

CORGI TOYS

In fact, Corgi Toys was certainly one of the more prolific manufacturers of Rover-inspired toys, starting with the No. 204 Rover 90 in 1956. More than 35,000 Rover 90s were produced between 1953 and 1959 and this top-end four-door saloon had a top speed of 90mph. Next from Corgi is the No. 252 Rover 2000, produced between 1963 and 1966. The following year, Corgi released the 2000 in Monte Carlo and International Rally finishes (No. 322) to give the car a suitably sporty finish. The later Rover 2000TC was available in 1968/71 with and without Corgi's innovative Take-Off Wheels.

ROVER P5 '3-LITRE'

Among the most detailed Rover replicas is certainly Spot-On's take on the Rover P5, badged as the '3-litre'. The real thing was launched in 1958 and production ceased in 1962, by which point more than 20,000 had been produced. Spot-On's take on the reliable runner was certainly up to its usual standard and was first released in 1963. Two versions were available, No. 157 and No. 157s, which came with lights.

ROVER 3500

Finally, for something a bit more modern and a fitting tribute to the Rover name, what about the Rover 3500, otherwise known as the SD1 – which referred to Special Division 1? The SD1 is often considered to be the last true Rover, as it was the final Rover-badged vehicle produced at the Solihull factory, as well as being the last car designed by Rover engineers and fitted with a V8 engine. Matchbox's Superfast take on this historic vehicle is simple enough but still captures the more modern angular shape of the 1976 vehicle. The last SD1 rolled off the production line in 1986 but the end was already in sight for Rover. ∎

ABOVE
The Rover 3500, the last true 'Rover' produced.

ABOVE
Morestone AA Road Service Land Rover, produced in the late 1950s.

Corgi Toys No. 333 Mini Cooper S RAC Rally, near excellent in excellent plus No. 225 box with 1966 RAC Rally white flash label with blue lettering. Sold for £140, Warwick & Warwick, September.

Corgi Toys No. 1121 Chipperfield's Circus Crane Truck, good to excellent in good to excellent lidded box with instructions and packing pieces. Sold for £75, Warwick & Warwick, September.

Corgi Toys Gift Set No. 4 Bristol Bloodhound, excellent to mint in good box, with packaging piece. Sold for £240, Warwick & Warwick, September.

Dinky Toys No. 111 Triumph TR2, with red hubs, excellent in near excellent box. Sold for £90, Warwick & Warwick, September.

Corgi Toys No. 322 Rover 2000 Monte Carlo, metallic maroon, red interior, excellent in excellent plus box (without leaflet). Sold for £100, Warwick & Warwick, September.

Corgi Toys No. 480 Chevrolet Impala Taxi, spun hubs, mint in excellent plus box with packing piece and Corgi Club leaflet. Sold for £80, Warwick & Warwick, September.

Dinky Toys No. 238 Jaguar D Type, turquoise, blue hubs, white driver, excellent in excellent box with Le Mans label. Sold for £85, Warwick & Warwick, September.

Dinky Toys No. 156 Rover 75, two tone light green/green, excellent in excellent box with correct colour spot. Sold for £140, Warwick & Warwick, September.

Dinky Toys No. 273 Mini Minor Van RAC, red interior, black base, about excellent in good plus box. Sold for £120, Warwick & Warwick, September.

Dinky Supertoys No. 901 Foden 8 Wheel Diesel Wagon, red cab, chassis and hubs, fawn back, generally good, some chipping to mudguards and front. In good box. Sold for £70, Warwick & Warwick, September.

Matchbox Regular Wheels No. 59a Ford Thames 'Singer' Van, pale green, grey plastic wheels, excellent plus in nearly excellent Type C Lesney box. Sold for £32, Warwick & Warwick, September.

Dinky Toys No. 280 Midland Mobile Bank, mint in an excellent box. Sold for £95, Cottees, September.

Dinky Toys No. 25x Commer Dinky Toy Service Breakdown Lorry, green cab and chassis, blue crane and housing with 'Dinky Service' to each side. Red ridged hubs. Sold for £70, Cottees, September.

Dinky Supertoys No. 561 Red Blaw Knox Bulldozer, red body and lifting blade with fawn driver and green tracks.Mint in an excellent plus blue box. Sold for £55, Cottees, September.

Corgi Toys No. 7 Massey Ferguson 65 Tractor and Tipper Trailer, boxed, good condition. Sold for £140, Hartleys, September.

Dinky Supertoys No. 923 Big Bedford Van 'Heinz', possible repaint, boxed, excellent condition. Sold for £130, Hartleys, September.

Dinky Supertoys No. 988 ABC TV Transmitter Van, boxed, good to excellent condition. Sold for £170, Hartleys, September.

Corgi Toys No. Marlin Rambler Sports Fastback, red, black, off-white interior, spun hubs, grey plastic tow hook. Mint in box. Sold for £100, Vectis, September.

Corgi Toys No. 264 Oldsmobile Tornado, blue body, pale cream interior, cast hubs, chrome front and rear bumpers. Mint in a near mint box. Sold for £90, Vectis, September.

Corgi Toys No. 327 MGB GT, red body, pale blue interior with black luggage case, wire wheels, chrome front and rear bumpers. Sold for £130, Vectis, September.

Dinky Toys No. 591 AEC Tanker 'Shell Chemicals Ltd.', overall very good, minor chips to occasional raised edges. Sold for £70, Sheffield Auction Gallery, September.

Corgi Toys No. 21 ERF Dropside Lorry and Platform Trailer, with millk churns, box acceptable to fair, no interior. Sold for £70, Hartleys, September.

Dinky Toys No. 941 Foden 14-ton Tanker 'Mobilgas', second type cab, boxed, good to excellent condition. Sold for £170, Hartleys, September.

Dinky Supertoys No. 986 Mighty Antar Low Loader with Propeller, boxed, fair to good condition. Sold for £160, Hartleys, September.

Corgi Toys No. 213 Jaguar 2.4 'Fire Service' Car, red body, flat spun hubs, grey plastic aerial, roof box. Mint in near mint blue and yellow carded box with leaflet. Sold for £120, Vectis, September.

Dinky Toys No. 344 Estate Car, in two tone brown. Very good plus. Boxed, with slight creasing to box. Sold for £75, Sheffield Auction Gallery, September.

Dinky Supertoys No. 514 Guy Van 'Lyons Swiss Rolls', overall good with signs of wear, small loss to part of transfer. Wear, fading, staining and rubbing to box. Sold for £150, Sheffield Auction Gallery, September.

Dinky Toys No. 252 Bedford Refuse Lorry, green, black tin shutters, cream wheels, windows. Overall good, minor chipping to raised edges. Sold for £180, Sheffield Auction Gallery, September.

Dinky Toys No. 942 Foden 14-Ton Tanker 'Regent', overall very good, slight staining and rubbing to box. Sold for £150, Sheffield Auction Gallery, September.

Dinky Supertoys No. 965 Euclid Rear Dump Truck, with windows. In very good conditon with minor chipping. Some wear to box. Sold for £60, Sheffield Auction Gallery, September.

Dinky Supertoys No. 960 Lorry Mounted Concrete Mixer, with windows, plastic wheels, overall very good condition. Boxed - some crushing, tear marks and rubbing to box. Sold for £50, Sheffield Auction Gallery, September.

Dinky Toys No. 165 Ford Capri, in purple. Very good plus. Boxed with some crushing/rub marks to box. Sold for £40, Sheffield Auction Gallery, September.

Dinky Toys No. 157 Jaguar XK 120 Coupe, red body, chrome spun hubs. Mint in excellent box with correct colour spot. Sold for £300, Vectis, September.

Dinky Toys No. 492 Loud Speaker Van, blue. Very good with odd chip. Staining to box. Sold for £45, Sheffield Auction Gallery, September.

Dinky Toys No. 153 Standard Vanguard Saloon, with mid blue body and cream hubs. Very good plus. Correct colour spot to box. Sold for £120, Sheffield Auction Gallery, September.

Corgi Toys No. 217 Fiat 1800, pale blue body, dark blue roof, lemon interior, flat spun hubs. Mint including blue/yellow carded picture box. Sold for £190, Vectis, September.

Corgi Toys No. 241 Ghia L.6.4., gold body, off-white interior, spun hubs, chrome front and rear bumpers. Harder to find variation. Sold for £200, Vectis, September.

Corgi Toys No. 330 Porsche Carrera 6, white body, red doors and bonnet with racing number 60, blue plastic engine cover, cast hubs, black interior with driver figure. Sold for £60, Vectis, September.

Corgi Toys No. 324 Marcos 1800GT, blue body, pale blue, cream interior with driver figure, wire wheels. Sold for £60, Vectis, September.

Dinky Toys No. 101 Sunbeam Alpine Sports Car maroon body, cream interior and ridged hubs, figure driver. Near mint. Sold for £170, Vectis, September.

Dinky Toys No. 105 Triumph TR2 Sports Car, lemon body, green interior with driver, spun hubs. Mint in box. Sold for £220, Vectis, September.

Dinky Toys No. 147 Cadillac 62, metallic green, factory finished dark green roof, red interior, chrome hubs - possible factory prototype or trial issue. Sold for £220, Vectis, September.

Dinky Toys No. 129 MG Midget Sports Car, US export issue, red body and ridged hubs, brown interior without driver figure. Excellent plus, unboxed. Sold for £480, Vectis, September.

Dinky Toys No. 136 Vauxhall Viva, metallic light blue, red interior, chrome hubs. Mint in near mint box. Sold for £70, Vectis, September.

French Dinky Toys No. 24V Buick Roadmaster, mid blue body, overall good plus with minor chipping. Some crushing and small tears to box. Sold for £110, Sheffield Auction Gallery, September.

Dinky Toys No. 178 Plymouth Plaza, with windows, dark blue roof to light blue body, spun hubs. Very good plus. Retailer's sticker, slight staining and crushing to box. Sold for £110, Sheffield Auction Gallery, September.

Dinky Toys No. 102 MG Midget Sports Car, pale green body, cream interior and ridged hubs, driver figure. Sold for £280, Vectis, September.

Dinky Toys No. 129 MG Midget Sports Car, US export issue, off-white, maroon interior, red hubs. Mint, unboxed. Sold for £320, Vectis, September.

Dinky Toys No. 152 Austin Devon Saloon, cerise lower body, green upper body, cream hubs. Mint in a generally good plus yellow carded picture box. Sold for £440, Vectis, September.

Dinky Toys No. 153 Standard Vanguard Saloon, maroon body and ridged hubs. Rare issue is generally mint in good plus box with correct colour spot. Sold for £1,600, Vectis, September.

Dinky Toys No. 181 Volkswagen Saloon, light blue body, chrome spun hubs. Mint including box. Sold for £90, Vectis, September.

Corgi Toys Whizzwheels No. 311 Ford Capri V6 3 litre, red body with Whizzwheels, black interior, in original yellow and orange Whizzwheels window box. Sold for £45, Lacy, Scott & Knight, August.

Corgi Toys No. 485 Mini Countryman with Surfer, sea-green body with lemon interior, chrome roof rack with 2 red surfboards, male standing figure, jewelled headlights, in the original all card blue and yellow box. Sold for £100, Lacy, Scott & Knight, August.

Dinky Toys No. 689 Medium Artillery Tractor, military green body with green tin rear canopy, with seated driver figures and green hubs, in original blue and white striped Supertoys box. Sold for £80, Lacy, Scott & Knight, August.

Corgi Toys No. 1120 Midland Red Motorway Express Coach, red body with black roof, flat spun hubs and Birmingham-London labels, lemon interior, black paint smudge above headlight, in original all card box with leaflet. Sold for £45, Lacy, Scott & Knight, August.

French Dinky No. 60C Lockheed Super-G Constellation, silver body with Air France transfers, F-BHBX to wings, 4x3 blade propellers, with original blue and white Supertoys box. Sold for £60, Lacy, Scott & Knight, August.

French Dinky No. 60E Dewoitine 500 Hunter, cream diecast body with open cockpit and tinplate wings, two-wheel undercarriage with two blade propeller, front and rear wings have red detailing, some losses. Sold for £90, Lacy, Scott & Knight, August.

Dinky Toys No. 412 Austin Wagon, blue body with lemon hubs, black and silver detailed grille, with hook, some playwear, model would require cleaning, correct colour spot box. Sold for £260, Lacy, Scott & Knight, August.

Dinky Toys No. 166 Renault R16, dark blue body with red seats, steering wheel and detailed grille, concave hubs, in the original white ground all card box. Sold for £65, Lacy, Scott & Knight, August.

Dinky Toys No. 109 Austin Healey 100 Sports Car, finished in yellow with blue interior, racing number 21, with driver and windscreen undamaged, some playwear in the original all card yellow box. Sold for £65, Lacy, Scott & Knight, August.

CIJ Peugeot Commerciale 403, boxed. Sold for £42, Reeman Dansie, September.

Dinky Toys No. 234 Ferrari Racing Car, boxed. Sold for £24, Reeman Dansie, September.

French Dinky No. 24V Buick Roadmaster, boxed. Sold for £32, Reeman Dansie, September.

Corgi Toys No. 339 BMC Mini Cooper 'S' 1967 Monte Carlo Winner, very good condition, some light wear, in very good box. Sold for £110, Aston's, August.

Dinky Toys No. 231 Maserati Racing Car, red, yellow plastic hubs with grey tyres, white flash and racing number nine. Near mint in excellent plus box. Sold for £200, Vectis, September.

Dinky Toys No. 234 Ferrari Racing Car, blue body, yellow triangle nose, bright yellow plastic hubs with grey tyres, yellow racing number five. Near mint in excellent box. Sold for £300, Vectis, September.

Dinky Toys No. 251 Aveling-Barford Road Roller, green, price sticker on roof, original box and insert. Sold for $80, Lloyd Ralston, August.

Solido No. 129 Ferrari Racer, red, original box. Sold for $210, Lloyd Ralston, August.

DIECAST   RAILWAYS   TOY FIGURES   TINPLATE   TV & FILM   OTHERS   EBUYS

Corgi Toys No. 484 Dodge 'Kew Fargo' Livestock Transporter with Animals, excellent in excellent box (slight rubbing to one end) with card packing piece and leaflet. Sold for £35, Cottees, September.

Corgi Toys No. 247 Mercedes Benz 600 Pullman, chrome trim, spun hubs, operative windscreen wipers, excellent in excellent box. Sold for £45, Cottees, September.

Dinky Toys Gift Set No. 4 Racing Cars, complete set, very good box. Sold for £380, Aston's, September.

Corgi Toys No. 241 Ghia L.6.4., Corgi dog on rear shelf, excellent (a few very tiny chips) in an excellent box with leaflet. Sold for £40, Cottees, September.

Corgi Toys No. 1106 Karrier Decca Mobile Radar Van, in original box with two packing pieces, very good to near mint, box very good. Sold for £140, Lacy, Scott & Knight, August.

French Dinky No. 60B Sud Aviation Vantour SNCA5O, metallic grey, twin jets on wings, blue cockpit with roundels to wings, in original all card yellow box, split to box corners. Sold for £45, Lacy, Scott & Knight, August.

Dinky Toys No. 615 US Jeep with 105mm Howitzer, US military green body, plastic wheels with grey plastic fittings, grey plastic driver, decals lifted on bonnet, with packing piece, inner pictorial display stand and box outer, sold with five pink shells. Sold for £90, Lacy, Scott & Knight, August.

French Dinky Toys No.541 Mercedes Benz Autocar, mid-red lower body with cream upper, clear glazing with light grey interior with chromed concave hubs, in the original pictorial all card box. Sold for £75, Lacy, Scott & Knight, August.

Dinky Toys No. 155 Ford Anglia, blue, original box. Sold for $90, Lloyd Ralston, August.

Dinky Toys No. 552 Chevy Corvair, box rub on roof, original box. Sold for $110, Lloyd Ralston, August.

Dinky Toys No. 430 Breakdown Lorry, tan and green, with windows, original box. Sold for $160, Lloyd Ralston, August.

Dinky Toys No. 455 Trojan Van Brooke Bond Tea, red, unboxed. Sold for $140, Lloyd Ralston, August.

Lone Star Roadmasters MG TF Model, light metallic aqua, black plastic interior, racing number seven decals, some paint loss to wheel edges otherwise excellent plus to near mint. Sold for £110, Vectis, August.

Corgi Toys No. 319 Lotus Elan Coupe, blue, white roof/interior, detachable chassis. Slight rub to roof otherwise near mint in good plus to excellent box. Sold for £45, Vectis, August.

Corgi Toys No. 211 Studebaker Golden Hawk, light blue, gold rear wing flash, smooth cast hubs. Good plus condition. Sold for £80, Vectis, August.

Corgi Toys No. 226 Morris Mini Minor, metallic maroon, pale yellow interior, detailed cast hubs, some minor marks but overall excellent. Sold for £50, Vectis, August.

Corgi Toys No. 411 Karrier Bantam Lucozade Van, yellow, silver trim, grey plastic shutter door, paper label decals to both sides, spun hubs. Sold for £110, Vectis, August.

Corgi Toys GS38 Monte Carlo Rally Gift Set, overall models are mint, outer card box is good to good plus. Sold for £750, Vectis, August.

Corgi Toys No. 217 Fiat 1800 pale blue body, dark blue roof, lemon interior, flat spun hubs. Mint including blue/yellow carded picture box. Sold for £190, Vectis, September.

Tri-ang Spot-On No. 154 Austin A40, in original box, very good to excellent condition, box good. Sold for £120, Special Auction Services, November.

Dinky Toys No. 166 Sunbeam Rapier, mint in a mint correctly colour coded box. Sold for £110, Cottees, November.

Corgi Toys No. 322 Rover 2000 Monte Carlo metallic maroon, red interior, excellent in excellent plus box (without leaflet). Sold for £100, Warwick & Warwick, September.

Dinky Toys No. 129 MG Midget Sports Car US export issue, red body and ridged hubs, brown interior without driver figure. Excellent plus, unboxed. Sold for £480, Vectis, September.

Matchbox Kingsize K-16 Dodge Tractor with Twin Tippers, green cab with green chassis, red plastic hubs with yellow tippers and Dodge Trucks transfers to sides, in original blue and yellow window box, window requires cleaning. Sold for £50, Lacy, Scott & Knight, August.

Corgi Toys No. 323 Citroen DS 19 in Monte Carlo trim,in original box with leaflet, very good to near mint, box very good. Sold for £260, Lacy, Scott & Knight, August.

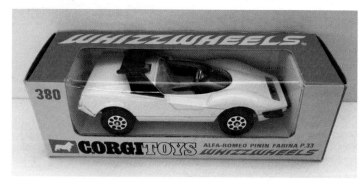

Corgi Toys No. 380 Alfa Romeo Pininfarina P.33,excellent in excellent/mint box with Corgi leaflet. Sold for £20, Cottees, September.

Corgi Toys No. 333 Mini Cooper S RAC Rally, near excellent in excellent plus No. 225 box with 1966 RAC Rally white flash label with blue lettering. Sold for £140, Warwick & Warwick, September.

Corgi Toys No. 216 Austin A40 Saloon, blue body, dark blue roof, flat spun hubs. Mint in a near mint blue/yellow carded picture box. Sold for £130, Vectis, September.

Corgi Toys No. 477 Red Land Rover Breakdown Truck, mint in a mint yellow and blue card picture box. Sold for £85, Cottees, November.

Dinky Toys No. 136 Vauxhall Viva, metallic light blue, red interior, chrome hubs. Mint in near mint box. Sold for £70, Vectis, September.

Uncommon Corgi Toys Morris Marina Coupe Whizzwheels, produced for British Leyland in standard BL orange, in an original box, believed to have been produced by Corgi for BL to give to customers, excellent, box very good. Sold for £950, Special Auction Services, November.

Corgi Major Toys Ford Tilt Cab 'H' Series with 'EXPRESS' Trailer, and detachable cab mint with figure in an excellent box with small repair to a corner edge. Sold for £75, Cottees, November.

Corgi Toys No. 1126 Ecurie Ecosse Racing Car Transporter, blue, silver trim, orange lettering to sides. Excellent in good plus to excellent lift off lid card box. Sold for £120, Vectis, August.

Corgi Toys GS3 RAF Land Rover and Missile on Trolley, near mint in fair to good card box. Sold for £110, Vectis, August.

Corgi Toys No. 435 Commer Wall's Refrigerator Van, mid blue cab, cream rear body with decals to both sides. Excellent plus to near mint. Sold for £80, Vectis, August.

Corgi Toys No. 241 Ghia L.6.4. gold body, off-white interior, spun hubs, chrome front and rear bumpers. Harder to find variation. Sold for £200, Vectis, September.

Dinky Toys No. 111 Triumph TR2, with red hubs, excellent in near excellent box. Sold for £90, Warwick & Warwick, September.

Dinky Toys No. 153 Standard Vanguard Saloon, maroon body and ridged hubs. Rare issue is generally mint in good plus box with correct colour spot. Sold for £1,600, Vectis, September.

Corgi Toys No. 352 RAF Staff Car Standard Vanguard, in the original all card blue box, with Corgi Model club leaflet, very good condition, box very good. Sold for £95, Lacy, Scott & Knight, November.

Dinky Toys No. 110 Aston Martin DB3 Sports Car racing number '22', in original box with correct colour spot, excellent condition, box good to very good. Sold for £100, Special Auction Services, November.

Dinky Toys No. 156 Rover 75, two tone light green/green, excellent in excellent box with correct colour spot. Sold for £140, Warwick & Warwick, September.

Corgi Toys No. 454 Commer Platform Lorry, in the original all card blue Corgi Toys box, with the original leaflet, near mint condition, box very good. Sold for £90, Lacy, Scott & Knight, November.

Corgi Toys No. 226 'Colman's Mustard Mania' Morris Mini Minor, rare promotional issue, with yellow body, cast hubs, in box with leaflet, excellent. Sold for £4,400, Special Auction Services, November.

Dinky Toys No. 238 Jaguar D Type, turquoise, blue hubs, white driver, excellent in excellent box with Le Mans label. Sold for £85, Warwick & Warwick, September.

Dinky Toys No. 105 Triumph TR2 Sports Car, lemon body, pale green interior with driver figure, spun hubs. Mint in box. Sold for £220, Vectis, September.

Dinky Toys No. 591 AEC Tanker 'Shell Chemicals Ltd.', overall very good, minor chips to occasional raised edges. Sold for £70, Sheffield Auction Gallery, September.

Corgi Toys Gift Set 47 Ford 5000, tractor and conveyor set in the original box and 2 Corgi Model Club leaflets, the box outer has been sellotape repaired, good condition, box good. Sold for £130, Lacy, Scott & Knight, November.

Dinky Toys No. 344 Estate Car, in two tone brown. Very good plus. Boxed, with slight creasing to box. Sold for £75, Sheffield Auction Gallery, September.

Dinky Toys No. 182 Porsche 356a Coupe, cerise body, chrome spun hubs, gloss black baseplate. Rare issue. Near mint in excellent plus box. Sold for £620, Vectis, September.

Corgi Toys No. 302 MGA Sports Car, in the original box with Corgi Club leaflet, very good condition, box very good. Sold for £85, Lacy, Scott & Knight, November.

Dinky Supertoys No. 901 Foden 8 Wheel Diesel Wagon, red cab, chassis and hubs, generally good, some chipping to mudguards and front. In good box. Sold for £70, Warwick & Warwick, September.

Dinky Toys No. 231 Maserati Racing Car, red, yellow plastic hubs with grey tyres, white flash and racing number nine. Near mint in excellent plus box. Sold for £200, Vectis, September.

Dinky Toys No. 234 Ferrari Racing Car, blue body, yellow triangle nose, bright yellow plastic hubs with grey tyres, yellow racing number five. Near mint in excellent box. Sold for £300, Vectis, September.

Corgi Toys No. 309 Aston Martin DB4 Competition Model, in the original all card yellow and blue box with Corgi Model Club leaflet, very good to near mint condition, box very good. Sold for £120, Lacy, Scott & Knight, November.

Tri-ang Spot-On No. 210/1 Morris Min Van 'Royal Mail', red body, off white interior, spun hubs, in original box, excellent condition, box fair to good. Sold for £120, Special Auction Services, November.

Corgi Toys No. 471 Smith's Karrier Mobile Canteen 'Joe's Diner', decal, in original box, excellent condition, box very good to excellent. Sold for £150, Special Auction Services, November.

Dinky Supertoys No. 923 Big Bedford Van 'Heinz', red cab and chassis, yellow back and hubs, in original box, very good condition, box fair. Sold for £130, Special Auction Services, November.

Dinky Supertoys No. 958 Snowplough, with windows. Very good condition. Boxed, minor rubbing to box, missing inserts. Sold for £85, Sheffield Auction Gallery, September.

Dinky Toys No. 102 MG Midget Sports Car, pale green body, cream interior and ridged hubs, driver figure. Sold for £280, Vectis, September.

Dinky Toys No. 930 Bedford Pallet-Jekta Van, finished in yellow with Dinky Toy livery. Complete with pallets. Front bumper repainted. Sold for £75, Sheffield Auction Gallery, September.

Tri-ang Spot-On No. 145 LT Route_master Bus route 284, 'Ovaltine' adverts, chrome radiator, in original box, very good condition, some minor corrosion marks to edges, box good to very good. Sold for £240, Special Auction Services, November.

Corgi Toys No. 151A Lotus Mark Eleven Le Mans, racing car in the original box with Corgi Model Club leaflet, near mint condition, box very good. Sold for £90, Lacy, Scott & Knight, November.

Corgi Toys No. 414 Bedford Dormobile Military Ambulance,in original box with leaflet, near mint, box very good. Sold for £120, Lacy, Scott & Knight, August.

Corgi Toys No. 411, Karrier Bantam Lucozade van, smooth hubs with paper label decals to both sides, in the original all card blue box with Corgi Model Club leaflet, very good condition, box good to very good. Sold for £170, Lacy, Scott & Knight, November.

Dinky Toys No. 514 Guy Van 'Spratts', red/cream 1st type cab and body, in original box, good condition, box fair to good. Sold for £130, Special Auction Services, November.

Corgi Toys No. 357 Military Land Rover,in original box with leaflet, near mint, box very good. Sold for £100, Lacy, Scott & Knight, August.

Corgi Toys No. 300 Chevrolet Corvette Stingray Coupe,excellent in excellent box (price in pen to front) with inner card and leaflet. Sold for £55, Cottees, September.

Dinky Supertoys No. 501 Foden Diesel 8-Wheel Wagon, 1st type pale grey cab and back, red flash and hubs, black chassis, no hook, herringbone tyres, in original box, very good condition, box passable. Sold for £230, Special Auction Services, November.

Corgi Toys No. 238 Jaguar Mark X, in near mint condition, couple of tiny paint chips to front wing, with an excellent box. Sold for £65, C&T Auctions, January.

Corgi Toys No. 455 Karrier Bantam Two Tonner, in near mint condition, with a superb early blue box and concertina leaflet. Sold for £75, C&T Auctions, January.

Spot-on ERF 68G, light turquoise, silver inner back and chassis, cast hubs. Good plus. Sold for £100, Vectis, February.

Spot-On No. 108 Triumph TR3 Sports Car, good plus to excellent. Sold for £110, Vectis, March.

Corgi Toys No. 210S Citroen DS19, in the original all card yellow and blue box, with the original Corgi Model Club leaflet, very good to near mint condition, box very good. Sold for £95, Lacy, Scott & Knight, November.

Dinky Supertoys No. 561 Red Blaw Knox Bulldozer, red body and lifting blade with fawn driver and green tracks. Mint in an excellent plus blue box. Sold for £55, Cottees, September.

Corgi Toys No. 334 Mini Cooper 'Magnifique', excellent in very good to excellent with pen to front end flap. Sold for £50, Cottees, September.

Dinky Toys No. 405 Universal Jeep, black windscreen with green ridged hubs, mint in a near mint correctly colour coded box. Sold for £70, Cottees, November.

Dublo Dinky Toys No. 73 Green Land Rover and Orange Horse Box Trailer, with black ramp and wheels, brown horse. Excellent plus in near mint picture box. Sold for £70, Cottees, September.

Dinky Toys No. 978 Refuse Wagon, excellent in very good box (pen and small tear to one end flap). Sold for £45, Cottees, September.

Dinky Supertoys No. 918 Guy Van 'Ever Ready', blue 2nd type cab, red hubs, spare wheel, in original box, very good, box good to very, lid date 12-55. Sold for £180, Special Auction Services, November.

Corgi Toys No. 202 Morris Cowley Saloon, in the original blue all card box, slight rubbing to roof, very good to near mint condition, box very good. Sold for £120, Lacy, Scott & Knight, November.

Budgie Toys No. 208 Army Green Personnel & Equipment Carrier, with sand coloured plastic hilt. Mint in an excellent box. Sold for £35, Cottees, September.

DIECAST   RAILWAYS   TOY FIGURES   TINPLATE   TV & FILM   OTHERS   EBUYS

Dinky Toys No. 435 Bedford TK Tipper, excellent in excellent box with card packing piece, price in pencil to one end. Sold for £50, Cottees, September.

Dinky Toys No. 448 Chevrolet Pick-Up & Trailers Set, about excellent and better in harder to find end flap picgture box, sellotape repairs to all flaps, otherwise good. Sold for £110, Warwick & Warwick, January.

Dinky Toys No. 913 Guy Flat Truck with Tailboard, nearly excellent in about good box, 'Joe' written on top and two sides. Sold for £100, Warwick & Warwick, January.

Corgi Toys No. 218 Aston Martin DB4, in original box with pen marks, very good, box very good. Sold for £70, Lacy, Scott & Knight, February.

Corgi Toys No. 201 Austin Cambridge Saloon, about mint in fair blue picture box. Sold for £100, Warwick & Warwick, January.

Dinky Toys No. 167 AC Aceca Coupe, nearly excellent in excellent box. Sold for £120, Warwick & Warwick, January.

Corgi Toys No. 351 Land Rover RAF Vehicle, in original box, some wear to end flaps, good to very good, box good. Sold for £50, Lacy, Scott & Knight, February.

Spot-on No. 120 Fiat Multipla, overall condition is generally excellent (does have a couple of small marks). In good carded box. Sold for £80, Vectis, February.

Dinky Toys No. 982 Pullmore Car Transporter, good plus in good 582/982 striped box, also with Loading Ramp No. 994 in box. Sold for £70, Warwick & Warwick, March.

Spot-On No. 112 Jensen 541, excellent plus, nice bright example in a generally good plus carded box (small tear to end flap), comes with folded leaflet and colour collectors card. Sold for £180, Vectis, March.

Corgi Toys Toys No. 314 Ferrari Berlinetta 250 Le Mans, in the original blue and yellow all card box, very good condition, box very good. Sold for £40, Lacy, Scott & Knight, November.

Corgi Toys Gift Set 13 Tour de France, in original window box, very good to excellent condition, box good to very good, minor creasing to cellophane. Sold for £180, Special Auction Services, November.

Corgi Toys No. 152S BRM Formula 1 Grand Prix Racing Car, excellent in very good box (small tear to inner end flap). Sold for £60, Cottees, September.

Tri-ang Spot-On No. 114 Jaguar 3.4 Litre, light blue body, cream interior, spun hubs, in original box, very good to excellent condition, box very good. Sold for £250, Special Auction Services, November.

Dinky Toys No. 236 Connaught Racing Car, about mint in good box. Sold for £75, Warwick & Warwick, January.

Corgi Toys No. 233 Heinkel Economy Car, kingfisher blue, mint including crisp blue and yellow box, with original pen mark to end. Sold for £260, Vectis, January.

Matchbox Regular Wheels No. 23c Bluebird Dauphine Caravan, metallic lime green, grey plastic wheels, mint in good plus scarce Type C Lesney box. Sold for £280, Warwick & Warwick, March.

Dinky Toys No. 162 Ford Zephyr Saloon, in near mint condition, with a very good box, correct colour spot on end flaps. Sold for £70, C&T Auctions, January.

Matchbox Regular Wheels No. 47b Commer Ice Cream Van 'Lyons Maid', blue body, white interior, roof ans side decals, gloss black clip fit base, 24-tread grey plastic wheels. Excellent in good later issue type E3 box for 'Lord Nielson' version. Sold for £140, Vectis, March.

Dinky Toys No. 450 Bedford TK Box Van, 'Castrol' in thick red letters, 'The Masterpiece in Oils' in white letters. About mint in nearly excellent box - one corner split. Sold for £85, Warwick & Warwick, January.

Dinky Toys No. 941 Foden 14-ton Tanker 'Mobilgas', nearly excellent in fair plus box. Sold for £160, Warwick & Warwick, January.

Corgi Toys No. 228 Volvo P1800, light salmon pink, mint including crisp blue and yellow box, with leaflet. Sold for £320, Vectis, January.

Corgi Toys No. 207M Standard Vanguard III Saloon, in near mint condition, with a very good box. Price label removed from one end. Sold for £120, C&T Auctions, January.

Dinky Toys No. 167 AC Aceca Coupe, with windows version, roof has been re-painted, some areas touched-in. Box very good. Sold for £40, Lacy, Scott & Knight, February.

Dinky Toys No. 255 Land Rover 'Mersey Tunnel Police', black smooth tyres, tow hook. Excellent with chips to front bumper, in generally good plus box. Sold for £40, Vectis, February.

Corgi Toys No. 226 Morris Mini-Minor, nearly mint in excellent picture box with price sticker on one end. Sold for £85, Warwick & Warwick, January.

Dinky Toys No. 133 Cunningham C-5R Road Racer, mottled base, some playwear, in original very crisp box. Good, box very good. Sold for £45, Lacy, Scott & Knight, February.

Tri-ang Spot-On No. 109/3 ERF 68g Dropside Lorry, good plus in good box with colour collectors card. Sold for £170, Warwick & Warwick, March.

Corgi Toys No. 259 'Le Dandy' Citroen Coupe, excellent in excellent box, one side faded with pencil mark. Sold for £70, Warwick & Warwick, January.

Corgi Toys No. 418 Austin London Taxi Cab, in near mint condition, with an excellent box and Corgi Club leaflet. Sold for £45, C&T Auctions, January.

Dinky Toys No. 174 Hudson Hornet Sedan, knobbly white tyres, overall condition is generally good plus, in a generally good plus to excellent yellow carded picture box with correct colour spot. Sold for £50, Vectis, February.

Spot-On No.119 Meadows Frisky, near mint (apart from small marks to roof) in a generally good plus box with correct colour spot. Sold for £80, Vectis, March.

Dinky Toys No. 197 Morris Mini-Traveller, excellent in nearly excellent box. Sold for £60, Warwick & Warwick, January.

Corgi Toys No. 417 Land Rover Breakdown Truck, in near mint condition, with excellent card box, inner packing and Corgi Club leaflet. Sold for £90, C&T Auctions, January.

Corgi Toys No. 255 Austin 60 De Luxe Saloon 'Corgi Motor School', rare variation fitted with No. 255 export left hand drive interior. Mint. Sold for £540, Vectis, January.

Dinky Toys No. 110 Aston Martin DB3, in the original correct colour spot box, one end flap missing and model is playworn. Sold for £40, Lacy, Scott & Knight, February.

Matchbox Models of Yesteryear Y5 1907 Peugeot Pre-production Colour Trial, missing roof and two wheels bend out of shape. Would benefit from cleaning. Sold for £190, Vectis, February.

Matchbox Regular Wheels No. 70b Ford D800 Grit Spreading Truck, lemon yellow container body with grey plastic slide. Overall near mint in near mint correct issue type F2 box. Sold for £120, Vectis, March.

Corgi Toys No. 316 NSU Sport Prinz, metallic rose red, near mint example of a harder to find colour variation. Sold for £260, Vectis, January.

Matchbox Regular Wheels No. 39c Ford Tractor, orange body, near mint in near mint correct late issue Superfast-style Type G box. Sold for £45, Vectis, March.

Matchbox Regular Wheels No. 65a Jaguar 3.4 Saloon, metallic blue body, gloss black base, plastic wheels with crimped axles. Mint apart from factory flaw to hood. Sold for £80, Vectis, March.

Spot-On No. 120 Fiat Multipla, near mint, beautiful example in a good box, with folded leaflet and colour collectors card. Sold for £220, Vectis, March.

Dinky Toys No. 155 Ford Anglia, excellent plus in excellent box. Sold for £65, Warwick & Warwick, January.

Corgi Toys No. 220 Chevrolet Impala, scarce spun wheels, in mint boxed condition. Superb example. Sold for £160, C&T Auctions, January.

Dinky Toys No. 942 Foden 14-ton Regent Tanker, red Supertoys hubs with Regent livery, playworn example in the original blue and white striped Supertoys box. Sold for £110, Lacy, Scott & Knight, February.

Spot-On No.131 Goggomobile Super, excellent, a nice bright example in a good plus box, with colour collectors card. Sold for £140, Vectis, March.

Dinky Toys No. 421 Electric Articulated Lorry, excellent plus in excellent box. Sold for £65, Warwick & Warwick, January.

Corgi Toys No. 200 Ford Consul Saloon, self adhesive accessories added, in excellent to near mint condition, some box rubbing. Sold for £70, C&T Auctions, January.

Dinky Toys No. 941 Foden 14-ton 'Mobilgas' Tanker, repainted, with original box. Sold for £110, Lacy, Scott & Knight, February.

Dinky Toys No. 340 Land Rover, with knobbly grey tyres, cream interior with driver figure, tow hook. Near mint in good plus to excellent yellow carded picture box with correct colour spot. Sold for £70, Vectis, February.

Spot-On No. 145 London Transport Routemaster Bus 'Drink Delicious Ovaltine the World's Best Nightcap', good plus in a good plus lift off lid box with some inner packing. Sold for £200, Vectis, March.

Dinky Supertoys No. 960 Albion Lorry Mounted Concrete Mixer, late example with black plastic wheels and light grey tyres, vehicle mint. In late-style picture box. Sold for £150, Wallis & Wallis, February.

Matchbox Superfast No. 62 Mercury Cougar Rat Rod Dragster, dark green body, silver painted base. Near mint in generally near mint type G box. Sold for £45, Vectis, February.

Dinky Toys No. 425 Bedford TK Coal Lorry, in red 'Hall & Co' livery, late example with red plastic wheels, complete with scales and coal sacks. Boxed, minor wear. Sold for £85, Wallis & Wallis, February.

DIECAST   RAILWAYS   TOY FIGURES   TINPLATE   TV & FILM   OTHERS   EBUYS

Matchbox Regular Wheels No. 25c Bedford TK Petrol Tanker 'Aral', dark blue cab and chassis, white tank, fine tread black plastic wheels. Excellent plus, few tiny chips to rear of tank, in fair Type E3 box. Sold for £110, Vectis, March.

Spot-On No. 165 Vauxhall Cresta, near mint, generally good plus box, which has flash. Sold for £220, Vectis, March.

Corgi Toys No. 218 Aston Martin DB4, excellent plus in excellent box. Sold for £80, Warwick & Warwick, January.

Corgi Toys No. 235 Oldsmobile Super 88, spun wheels, in mint boxed condition. Sold for £80, C&T Auctions, January.

Dinky Toys No. 210 Alfa-Romeo 33 Tipo Le Mans, in original plastic hard case with instruction leaflet. Very good. Sold for £55, Lacy, Scott & Knight, February.

Dinky Toys No. 919 Guy 'Robertson's Golden Shred' Van, good plus to excellent, in good plus box. Sold for £400, Vectis, January.

Matchbox Suerfast No. 9 AMX Javelin, red body with cast shut doors, amber windows, dark yellow interior, silver painted base, five-arch wheels. Near mint. Sold for £60, Vectis, February.

Corgi Major Toys No. 1105 'Carrimore' Car Transport with a Bedford Tractor Unit, boxed, splitting to two corners. Vehicle very good condition, a few minor chips. Sold for £65, Wallis & Wallis, February.

Dinky Toys No. 40J Austin Somerset Saloon, nearly good in good plus box, with correct colour spot. Sold for £70, Warwick & Warwick, March.

Spot-On No. 216 Volvo 122S with sliding roof, excellent plus in a generally excellent picture box with colour collectors card. Sold for £340, Vectis, March.

Corgi Toys No. 443 Plymouth Sport Suburban Station Wagon 'US Mail', mint apart from a couple of minor factory marks, in mint box. Sold for £180, Vectis, January.

Corgi Toys No. 231 Triumph Herald Coupe, spun wheels, in near mint boxed condition. Sold for £90, C&T Auctions, January.

Matchbox No. 17 Bedford Removals Van, in original B-type all-card box, very good to near mint, box good to very good. Sold for £40, Lacy, Scott & Knight, February.

Matchbox Superfast Twin Pack Series Articulated Petrol Tanker Pre-production Colour Trial, black tractor unit base with incomplete copyright date, white plastic tank (discoloured). Sold for £280, Vectis, February.

Spot-On No. 267 MG 1100 with opening bonnet, excellent plus, beautiful example in a generally good presentation window box, inner carded tray is good plus. Sold for £220, Vectis, March.

Corgi Toys No. 208S Jaguar 2.4 litre Saloon, excellent plus in good plus box with Corgi Model Club leaflet. Sold for £85, Warwick & Warwick, January.

Matchbox No. 12 Land Rover, tan driver with metal wheels, in original B-type all-card box. Very good to near mint, box good to very good. Sold for £40, Lacy, Scott & Knight, February.

Matchbox Regular Wheels No. 74b Daimler Fleetline Bus, promotional issue, cream body with 'Presidential Weekend Sheffield June 1967' labels. Excellent with some small paint chips. Unusual Code 3 issue. Sold for £80, Vectis, February.

Matchbox Regular Wheels No. 20c Chevrolet Impala Taxi, orange-yellow body with hood decal, bare metal issue, 36-tread grey plastic wheels. Excellent in excellent later issue Type E4 box. Sold for £800, Vectis, March.

Dinky Toys No. 189 Promotional Triumph Herald, example in white with Monaco blue roof and lower sides. With spun wheels and no interior. Very good condition, minor wear/light chips. Sold for £300, Wallis & Wallis, February.

Budgie No. 278 Land Rover 'RAC Radio Rescue', overall condition is near mint (roof does have slight warping) in a generally good plus picture box. Sold for £190, Vectis, February.

Corgi Toys No. 436 Citroen Safari ID19 'Wildlife Preservation', mint in mint blue and yellow box, with leaflet. Sold for £130, Vectis, January.

Corgi Toys No. 227 Morris Mini Cooper Competition Model, in original box, racing number seven, some losses, good condition, box good. Sold for £65, Lacy, Scott & Knight February.

Corgi Toys No. 256 East African Safari VW 1200, excellent plus in good plus picture box. Sold for £120, Warwick & Warwick, January.

Corgi Toys Farming Gift Set No. 9 with Massey Ferguson 165 Tractor with shovel and tipping trailer, excellent plus in good plus picture box, with excellent inner pictorial stand. Sold for £95, Warwick & Warwick, January.

Matchbox K-23 King Size Mercury Police Car, in original blue and yellow window with un-folded header card. Very good, box very good. Sold for £20, Lacy, Scott & Knight, February.

Matchbox Superfast No. 32 Leyland Tanker 'Aral', chrome grille and base, good plus in good box. Sold for £80, Vectis, February.

Matchbox Regular Wheels No. 46b Guy Pickfords Removal Van, dark blue type B detailed body, two-line decals, gloss black base, 20-tread grey plastic wheels. Excellent plus in excellent Type D1 box. Sold for £60, Vectis, March.

DIECAST   RAILWAYS   TOY FIGURES   TINPLATE   TV & FILM   OTHERS   EBUYS

Lone Star Flyers No. 7 Vauxhall Firenza, good plus to excellent, has small chips around front and rear edges. In good plus to excellent box. Sold for £120, Vectis, February.

Corgi Toys No. 222 Renault Floride, mint including crisp blue and yellow box with folded leaflet. Sold for £140, Vectis, January.

Spot-on Hillman Minx, dull green, red interior, complete with luggage rack and two brown cases. Near mint. Sold for £80, Vectis, February.

Corgi Toys No. 328 Monte Carlo 1966 Hillman Imp, in original box, very good, box good to very good. Sold for £110, Lacy, Scott & Knight, August.

Spot-On No. 110/4 AEC Mammoth Major 8 4000 Gallon Auto Petrol Tanker, rare and hard to find issue, generally near mint in a generally excellent lift off lid box with over label to end. Sold for £1,400, Vectis, March.

Dinky Toys No. 172 Studebaker Land Crusier, excellent plus in nearly excellent box. Sold for £80, Warwick & Warwick, January.

Corgi Toys No. 318 Lotus Elan S2 'I've got a Tiger in my Tank', mint example, complete with racing number five unapplied decals. Sold for £640, Vectis, January.

Corgi Toys No. 247 Mercedes Benz 600 Pullman, with instruction leaflet, in mint boxed condition. Sold for £160, C&T Auctions, January.

Matchbox 1-75 Series No. 32 Jaguar XK140, white body with metal wheels, in original Moko B-type box, requires cleaning. Fair to good, box good. Sold for £30, Lacy, Scott & Knight, February.

Matchbox Superfast No. 26 GMC Tipper Truck, factory error wheel variation, spiro wheels fitted to front axle, standard issue four-spoke wheels fitted to rear. Excellent plus. Sold for £150, Vectis, February.

Matchbox Regular Wheels No. 74a Mobile Refreshments Canteen, deep cream body, mid-blue base and interior, 20-tread grey plastic wheels. Excellent, unboxed. Sold for £60, Vectis, March.

Spot-On No. 210/1 Mini Van 'Royal Mail', excellent plus in a generally good plus to excellent picture box. Sold for £200, Vectis, March.

Dinky Toys No. 435 Bedford TK Tipper, excellent plus in nearly excellent box. Sold for £55, Warwick & Warwick, January.

Corgi Toys No. 225 Austin 7 Mini, mint in a near mint blue and yellow box, pen mark to end flap. Sold for £130, Vectis, January.

Corgi Toys Gift Set 37 Lotus Racing Team, includes accessories, bollards and paperwork. Boxed, minor wear. Contents very good to mint. Sold for £65, Wallis & Wallis, February.

Matchbox No. 73B Ferrari F1 Racing Car, with spoked metal hubs, in the original D-type picture box, pierced to one end flap. Good to very good, box good. Sold for £20, Lacy, Scott & Knight, February.

Dinky Supertoys No. 504 Foden 14 Ton Tanker, first type cab, good/ good plus in good plus box. Sold for £160, Warwick & Warwick, January.

Corgi Toys No. 240 Ghia Fiat 600 Jolly, mint in a near mint box with leaflet, pen mark to box. Sold for £220, Vectis, January.

Matchbox No. 53A Aston Martin DB2-4 Mk1, metal wheels and silver detailing, in original enlarged B-type box. Very good, box good. Sold for £45, Lacy, Scott & Knight, February.

Matchbox Superfast No. 22 Pontiac GP Coupe, metallic dark purple body without silver grille, black base, five-spoke narrow wheels. Mint in fair type G box. Sold for £110, Vectis, February.

Matchbox Regular Wheels No. 32a Jaguar XK140, red body with mask sprayed front silver trim, gloss black base, 20-tread grey plastic wheels with rounded axles. Mint apart from minor factory paint flaw to base, in good Type C Lesney box. Sold for £70, Vectis, March.

Corgi Toys No. 233 Heinkel Economy Car, flat spun wheels, with Corgi leaflet, mint. Sold for £90, C&T Auctions, January.

Corgi Toys No. 472 Land Rover Public Address Vehicle 'Vote for Corgi', mint in a near mint box. Sold for £260, Vectis, January.

Budgie No. 282 Euclid 21 Yard Scraper, mint in a near mint (factory sealed) presentation window box. Sold for £200, Vectis, February.

Read in-depth **diecast features** every month in **Collectors Gazette** only £3.25

Dinky Toys No. 181 Volkswagen Saloon, lime green body, excellent plus in nearly excellent box with correct colour spot. Sold for £100, Warwick & Warwick, March.

Corgi Toys No. 210 Citroen DS19, near mint with a very minor roof mark, in mint crisp blue and yellow box, with folded Collectors Club leaflet. Sold for £100, Vectis, January.

Spot-on Bedford 'Shell Petroleum Products BP' Tanker, turquoise cab with black chassis, red tanker, black gantry, cast hubs. Good, unboxed. Sold for £160, Vectis, February.

Corgi Toys No. 458 ERF Earth Dumper, near mint, including crisp box. Sold for £60, Vectis, January.

Pre-War Dinky Toys No. 28a 'Hornby Trains' Delivery Van, fair condition, transfers clean and bright, small hole in radiator, paint loss to front mudguards and scratches to roof. Sold for £440, Special Auction Services, July.

Tri-ang Spot-On No.106A/OC Austin Articulated Flatbed Lorry, in original box, good, set lacks MGA and flatbed lacks headboard, box fair. Sold for £180, Special Auction Services, July.

Corgi Toys No. 242 Ghia Fiat 600 Jolly, excellent plus in a generally good plus to excellent box (small pencil price mark to end flap). Sold for £280, Vectis, August.

Corgi Toys No. 416 RAC Radio Rescue Land Rover, with original box. Sold for £40, Stroud Auctions, May.

Corgi Toys No. 462 Promotional Commer Van for Hammonds, in box with pencil '462' on ends, near mint, box near mint. Sold for £210, Lacy, Scott & Knight, May.

Matchbox Superfast No.4a Dodge Stake Truck, rare lemon yellow cab and chassis, mint apart from two tiny chips, in good plus 'new' type G box. Sold for £130, Vectis Auctions, June.

Dinky Toys No. 295 Standard Atlas, scarce example in all over light blue with red interior, boxed, minor wear. Vehicle very good to mint condition. Sold for £100, Wallis & Wallis, April.

Tri-ang Spot-On No.158A/2 Bedford Shell BP Tanker, in original box, good to very good, cab lacks coupling, tank lacks ladder, box passable with tape repairs. Sold for £250, Special Auction Services, July.

French Dinky No. 1420 Opel Commodore, silvered wheels with black tyres, boxed, minor wear/marking. Vehicle in very good condition wth minor chips only. Sold for £60, Wallis & Wallis, April.

Corgi Toys No. 275 Rover 2000TC, rare variant, white with maroon interior and amber roof panel, window box with diorama, mint, box near mint. Sold for £140, Lacy, Scott & Knight, May.

Pre-War Dinky Toys No. 33r Railway Mechanical Horse & Trailer Van, SR 'Southern Railway' livery, very good, minor fatigue signs to hubs, cream paint crazed. Sold for £260, Special Auction Services, July.

Tri-ang Spot-On No.109/3 ERF 68G Dropside Lorry, in original box, good, box passable to fair, lid split at corners. Sold for £180, Special Auction Services, July.

Corgi Toys Gift Set 6 Volkswagen Breakdown Truck with Trailer and Cooper-Maserati F1, in original box. Sold for £130, Stroud Auctions, May.

Corgi Toys No. 323 Citroen DS19, in Monte Carlo trim, suspension, tiny chip on roof, with club leaflet, near mint, box near mint. Sold for £320, Lacy, Scott & Knight, May.

Pre-War Dinky Toys No. 24e Super Streamlined Saloon, plated 'Tootsie Toy' type hubs, good, fatigue throughout, minor glue repair to rear wheel arch. Sold for £150, Special Auction Services, July.

Corgi Toys No. 251 Hillman Imp, near mint (very minor box rub wear marks to roof) in a good plus box with leaflet. Sold for £60, Vectis, August.

Matchbox Superfast No.5a Lotus Europa, bare metal base, five-spoke narrow wheels, mint in good 'new' type G box. Sold for £25, Vectis Auctions, June.

Corgi Toys Gift Set 48 Car Transporter with Six Car, with Automatic Coupling Ford 'H' Series Tilt Cab and all six cars, in original box. Sold for £240, Stroud Auctions, May.

Matchbox 55B1 Ford Fairlane Police Car, original box. Sold for $130, Lloyd Ralston, June.

Dinky Toys US Issue No. 39eu Chrysler Royal Sedan, very good to excellent, minor re-touching to nose, roof corner and rear wheel arch. Sold for £440, Special Auction Services, July.

Corgi Toys No. 263 Marlin Rambler Sports Fastback, mint in a generally excellent plus box with leaflet. Sold for £60, Vectis, August.

Matchbox Superfast No.7c Volkswagen Golf, mint apart from a couple of tiny factory assembly chips to base in good plus type K box. Sold for £40, Vectis Auctions, June.

Tri-ang Spot-On No.264 Tourist Caravan, in original box with two yellow packing pieces, very good to excellent, requires cleaning, box fair. Sold for £130, Special Auction Services, July.

Corgi Toys No. 202 Morris Cowley Saloon, in original all-card blue box with leaflet, near mint, box very good. Sold for £110, Lacy, Scott & Knight, May.

Pre-War Dinky Toys No. 28h Delivery Van 'Dunlop', type 2, good, fatigue in places, window strut and cracks glue repaired. Sold for £360, Special Auction Services, July.

Tri-ang Spot-On No.304 Volkswagen Variant, excellent, lacks skis and poles. Sold for £360, Special Auction Services, July.

Corgi Toys No. 259 Le Dandy Coupe, near mint (does require very slight cleaning) in a good plus box with leaflet. Sold for £60, Vectis, August.

Tekno No. 826 Ford Taunus 17M, pale greyish blue, silver trim - overall condition is generally excellent plus, nice bright example in a good plus carded box. Sold for £70, Vectis, June.

Corgi Toys No. 340 Sunbeam Imp Rally, car has weak springs, over-labelled box. Sold for $150, Lloyd Ralston, June.

Matchbox Superfast No.5b Seafire Power Boat, mint in near mint 'new' type J box with turquoise background print. Sold for £60, Vectis, June.

Corgi Toys No. 200 Ford Consul Saloon, in original blue all-card box with leaflet and Corgi Model Club pink leaflet, near mint, box very good. Sold for £120, Lacy, Scott & Knight, May.

Corgi Toys No. 485 BMC Mini Countryman, surfer, two maroon surfboards, excellent plus in excellent plus box with Corgi Model Club leaflet. Sold for £120, Warwick & Warwick, May.

Corgi Toys No.210s Citroen DS19, red body, lemon interior, silver trim, flat spun hubs. Excellent plus, bright example in a good to good plus blue and yellow carded picture box. Sold for £60, Vectis, June.

Corgi Toys No. 1126 Ecurie Ecosse Racing Car Transporter, original box and insert. Sold for $320, Lloyd Ralston, June.

Corgi Toys No. 205 Riley Pathfinder Saloon, in original blue all-card box with leaflet, near mint, box very good. Sold for £110, Lacy, Scott & Knight, May.

Corgi Toys No. 236 Corgi Motor School, turning wheel in working order, in the original blue and yellow all-card box with leaflet, near mint, box very good. Sold for £85, Lacy, Scott & Knight, May.

Corgi Toys No. 213S Jaguar Fire Service Car, mint in good plus box with leaflet. Sold for £80, Warwick & Warwick, July.

Dinky Supertoys No. 948 McLean Tractor-Trailer, in original box, very good to excellent, box very good. Sold for £120, Special Auction Services, July.

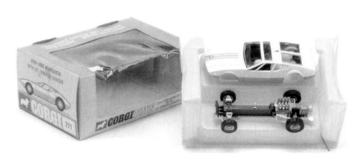

Corgi Toys No. 271 Ghia 5000 Mangusta with De Tomaso Chassis, overall condition appears to be generally near mint, inner plastic tray is excellent in a good plus box. Sold for £60, Vectis, August.

Dinky Toys No. 504 Foden Mobilgas Tanker, good, some foxing to black filler caps and paint chips to step and wheel arches, box fair. Sold for £110, Special Auction Services, July.

Dinky Toys No. 31d Trojan 'Beefy OXO', good plus, still a nice bright example. Sold for £70, Vectis, June.

Dinky Toys No. 107 Sunbeam Alpine Sports, good plus in fair box with correct colour spot. Sold for £60, Warwick & Warwick, July.

Corgi Toys No. 302 MGA Sports Car, mint (a couple of very minor marks to front and rear bumpers), in a generally good plus box. Sold for £110, Vectis, August.

French Dinky No. 512 Leskokert Midjet Cart, blue with harded to find driver dressed in red jacket. Near mint in a fair carded picture box. Sold for £60, Vectis, May.

Dinky Toys No. 666 Missile Erecting Vehicle with Corporal Missile, with instructions, in original box with two inserts, good, lacks launching platform, box good. Sold for £60, Special Auction Services, July.

Corgi Toys No. 323 Citroen DS19 "Rallye Monte Carlo", excellent (although does have some light Superdetailing) in a generally good plus to excellent blue and yellow carded picture box with Collectors Club folded leaflet. Sold for £120, Vectis, June.

Matchbox 565B3 Fiat 1500, orginal but worn box. Sold for $80, Lloyd Ralston, June.

Matchbox Superfast No.8a Ford Mustang, excellent plus in good type F transitional box. Sold for £120, Vectis, June.

Corgi Toys No. 215S Ford Thunderbirds Open Sports, in original blue and yellow all-card box with leaflet, near mint, box very good. Sold for £90, Lacy, Scott & Knight, May.

Dinky Toys No. 452 Trojan Chivers Jellies Van, unboxed, good plus. Sold for £40, Warwick & Warwick, May.

Corgi Toys No. 226 Morris Mini Minor, mint in good plus box with leaflet. Sold for £60, Warwick & Warwick, July.

Corgi Toys No. 273 Rolls Royce Silver Shadow, cast Golden Jacks take-off wheels, near mint in a generally excellent window box. Sold for £50, Vectis, August.

Corgi Toys No. 310 Chevrolet Corvette Stingray, in near mint condition, with a good box complete with end flaps. Sold for £50, C&T Auctions, July.

Matchbox Superfast No.9a Cabin Cruiser & Trailer Twin Pack Issue, near mint (chip to foot of towing eye) in mint 'new' type G box. Sold for £160, Vectis, June.

Corgi Toys No. 301 Triumph TR2 Sports Car, in original blue and yellow all-card box with leaflet, near mint, box very good. Sold for £150, Lacy, Scott & Knight, May.

Corgi Toys No. 151A Lotus XI Le Mans Racing Car, in original box, near mint, box very good. Sold for £95, Lacy, Scott & Knight, August.

Dinky Toys No. 137 Plymouth Fury Convertible, in mint condition, with an excellent box. Sold for £90, C&T Auctions, July.

Corgi Toys No. 259 Citroen Le Dandy, excellent In good plus box. Sold for £32, Warwick & Warwick, May.

Corgi Toys No. 302 MGA Sports Car, in original blue and yellow all-card box with leaflet, very good, box very good. Sold for £140, Lacy, Scott & Knight, May.

Corgi Toys No. 441 Volkswagen 'Chocolate Toblerone' van, in original blue and yellow all-card box with model club leaflet, good to very good, box very good. Sold for £100, Lacy, Scott & Knight, May.

Corgi Toys No. 314 Ferrari 250 Le Mans Berlinetta, near mint in a generally good plus to excellent box. Sold for £60, Vectis, August.

Corgi Toys No. 249 Morris Mini Cooper, with deluxe wicker work, in original blue and yellow all-card box with leaflet, very good to near mint, box very good. Sold for £140, Lacy, Scott & Knight, May.

Corgi Toys No. 307 'E' Type Jaguar, with detachable hard-top, cardboard packing ring and club leaflet, in yellow and blue box, near mint to mint, box near mint. Sold for £120, Lacy, Scott & Knight, May.

Dinky Toys No. 265 Plymouth Plaza USA "Taxi" excellent bright example in a generally excellent yellow carded picture box. Sold for £90, Vectis Auctions, June.

Dinky Toys No. 532 Leyland Comet Lorry, Supertoy hubs with grey treaded tyres. Good plus still a nice bright example of a harder issue to find. Sold for £70, Vectis, June.

Dinky Toys No. 675 US Army Staff Car, in original plain box, very good, box good. Sold for £140, Special Auction Services, July.

Dinky Toys No. 25x Breakdown Lorry, in original orange picture box, excellent, box good. Sold for £200, Special Auction Services, July.

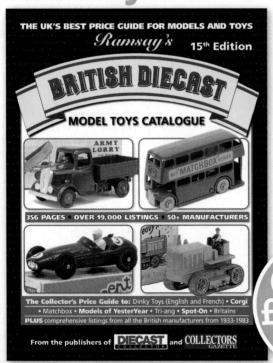

DIECAST   RAILWAYS   TOY FIGURES   TINPLATE   TV & FILM   OTHERS   EBUYS

Introduction to Model Railways

Collecting model railways is one of the oldest areas of the hobby, with some locomotives dating back to the middle of the 19th century.

To someone who doesn't collect model railways, this is one of those categories that can often seem a confusing jumble of random numbers, letters and references, e.g. Wrenn Railways OO gauge W2210 LNER blue 4-6-2 with tender. Compared to the fairly simple diecast descriptions, that tend to just have the manufacturer and vehicle model as a name, a replica loco is a little more complicated.

Of course, when you break it all down, then there's really nothing to be confused about and most descriptions include: manufacturer, scale of the model, locomotive number, railway company and the way the wheels are positioned on the actual locomotive. All that will come in handy when you're trying to work out if the model you've got at home, is the same as one of the ones listed here – again, that'll be useful if you're picking up this annual for the first time.

Rather like diecast, model locomotives, carriages, coaches and the numerous accessories associated with them are another staple at auction houses around the world. Then again, you can understand why, as the first toy locomotives were released in the 19th century, ensuring that generations have grown up playing with them during their formative years. Some of the first were produced in Germany by manufacturers like Bing or Marklin but were large, clockwork affairs made from tinplate. For something a little more fancy, then there was the option to pick up oil-fired examples that moved on their own steam, so to speak. Unfortunately, these had a reputation for leaking oil on the carpet, which earned them the nickname 'dribblers'.

From these humble beginnings model locomotives became a huge industry, particularly in the UK where Frank Hornby (the creator of Meccano) helped to establish the Hornby brand as a household name. Ask anyone in the street if they know what Hornby makes and the chances are they'll say 'toy trains'. With Hornby leading the way, other UK companies followed the charge and over the next few pages you'll come across other brands like Wrenn or Bassett-Lowke who have become equally collectable as Hornby and, in some cases, are actually worth more than the O gauge or OO products from the famous Liverpool-based firm.

Along with the locomotives themselves, there's a healthy market for the numerous accessories produced to accompany a layout. Whether you want a particular coach or goods wagon, then the chances are someone will have produced the item you're after. What's more, some of these can command high prices too and it's not just the glitzy locomotives that get all the attention at auction, as you'll see. Likewise, there are plenty of buildings or figures to place around your layout and some of the tinplate buildings from German companies like Marklin or even our own Hornby are particularly exquisite.

However, perhaps the best thing about these vintage locomotives is having the opportunity to see them running at shows or events around the country. There are even a few museums, like the stunning Brighton Toy Museum that have permanent displays for you to enjoy. ∎

233
You'll find 233 locomotives, coaches, wagons and sets in this section.

1863
Frank Hornby was born in 1863 and died in 1936.

£153
A quick bit of maths, shows this year's average price is £153.

£750
Our highest price this year is for an uncommon Hornby-Dublo set.

£35,774
The total amount for the railways category is £35,774.

Trackside by the seaside

We remember 60 years of model railways in Margate.

Mention Margate to someone in the street and they'll probably think of buckets and spades, amusement arcades and, if they watch episodes of The Only Way is Essex, copious amounts of fake tan. However, mention Margate to a model railway enthusiast and you might get a different reaction, as their eyes glaze over and they think of the output of world renowned model railway manufacturer Hornby, which is based in the seaside town. The factory has been an iconic fixture on the Margate landscape for 60 years but it didn't always say Hornby above the entrance...

To trace the origins of the factory we must travel back to 1946 when the green shoots of present-day Hornby were sprouting from a company called Rovex Plastics Ltd. Founded by Mr. Venetzian in 1946 and based in Chelsea, Rovex began making high quality plastic toys for Marks and Spencer, including a doll's tea set, telephone, speedboat and racing car. The success of these initial items (these are not just toys... these are M&S toys) led M&S to commission an ambitious electric railway from Rovex. Once again, it proved to be a huge success but just when Rovex was gearing up to begin full production, restrictions on the use of non-ferrous metal by the government for the Korean War, plus the need for more capital, meant that Venetzian sold the Rovex company to Tri-ang (Lines Bros.) in October 1951, who renamed it Rovex Scale Models Ltd.

Production now moved to a

No, this isn't a laboratory full of mad scientists, this is the old tool room.

larger factory in Richmond so that Tri-ang could keep up with the demand for train sets and accessories (extra track, points, goods wagons, etc). However, by the middle of the 1950s it soon became clear that even these bigger premises were not large enough to meet demand and the hunt was on for a suitable site

elsewhere, close enough to London but without the high overheads of working in the capital. As the Hornby Book of Trains puts it: "finally Margate was selected as offering an excellent site, good labour and an enthusiastic and helpful local council".

The site was actually purchased at the end of 1953 and work began

straight away. It was designed so that production flowed from one side to the other, so that if an extension was ever needed at the rear, it could be built without interfering with the existing layout. The first machines were moved into the building in May, with production planned to start in June. During this time every

ABOVE Forget computers, back in the 1960s all the models were designed and drawn by hand.

ABOVE The machine shop in 1962. *Tri-ang Railways: The First 10 Years.*

ABOVE Aerial view of the Hornby building in 1962 - although then it was known as the Rovex factory.

ABOVE Employees busy working in the despatch department.

weekend saw the arrival of more machinery from the existing Richmond plant, until the move was completed in October. However, the move wasn't without its problems. In the 1950s, London was a hive of manufacturing and there were skilled works and engineers able to try their hand at model railways... but in Margate skilled toolmakers were in short supply. As a result, new workers had to be trained up, which slowed progress slightly.

One of the busiest departments in the early days would have certainly been the Service Department, which handled repairs for customers. In Tri-ang Railways: The First 10 Years, the author goes into great depth explaining how repairs were handled by the factory at this time, even noting that all the paper documents that came with the model would be kept, just in case the owner needed to be traced at a later date by looking at the postmark. It's also noted how the service engineer would test absolutely everything on the locomotive and if further problems were found, he would then write to the owner to check if he wanted them fixing. Imagine getting that kind of service now!

The book points out: "The Service Department is proud of its thoroughness and in checking all items sent in; and also of the speed with which they were returned. During the slack period of the summer, most servicing jobs are completed within 24 hours of being received... we know what it feels like to be without a much-loved locomotive!" However, by the 1960s, this department was struggling to keep up with the huge demand, so the Service Dealer Scheme was launched, which saw retailers fixing broken locos, rather than sending them off to Margate.

Everything was handled at the factory, from initial design through to the manufacturing and shipping. In Tri-ang Railways: The First 10 Years, the sheer scale of the operation is highlighted: "there are bins containing some 1,800 different components which go up to make Tri-ang Railways. In one of those bins, last time we looked, were 1,884,734 axles. That gives you some idea of what is meant when we say that the home of Tri-ang Railways is one of the biggest factories of its kind in the world."

There were hundreds of jobs in the factory including: making injection mouldings, compression mouldings, metal pressings, diecastings, turnings, wire forms and sintered components. The staff would mould, cast, press, form, drill, tap, mill and turn; spray-paint, varnish, line, blacken, nickel-plate, stove-enamel, transfer and heat print. And this is before they're even assembled! However, it was quite a modern place to work, as the Tri-ang Railways book points out: "Some things [stand out]. One is the great size of the enterprise. Another is how clean and light and airy the factory is – a most pleasant place to work in. So it is no surprise to hear the girls suddenly burst out singing."

In fact, by 1962 Tri-ang had produced the equivalent of 9,000 miles of track and at least one piece of track was being manufactured every second. A couple of years later in 1964, we saw one of the biggest changes for Tri-ang, as it bought up the struggling Meccano company, which had been producing model railways under the Hornby name since the 1920s. It then changed its named to Tri-ang Hornby the following year.

Sadly in 1971 the previously all-conquering Lines Bros. went into receivership, plunging Tri-ang Hornby into potential peril. Thankfully the company was snapped up in 1972 by the little known Dunbee-Combex-Marx who quickly set about reviving the ailing fortunes, as well as changing the name from Tri-ang Hornby to just Hornby. Dunbee-Combex-Marx quickly set about rescuing the company and ramped up production in Margate, likewise long-shelved plans to build a substantial warehouse on adjacent land were finally put into production.

Unfortunately the next milestone in Hornby's history sounded the death knell for model manufacture in Margate. In 1999 Hornby – now trading as Hornby Hobbies Ltd – sacked more than 400 workers and moved production to China, leaving the factory as an almost empty shell that was used for storage. Up until recently a skeleton staff of sales and marketing were based at the Margate HQ but now they've been moved too, leaving behind the Hornby Visitor Centre, which is still worth a visit to celebrate the building's past. ∎

The 'L' word

We discover one of the more unusual gauges of model railways as we look into the history of LEGO Trains.

I f you're a model railway collector, it's more than likely you've heard of the various gauges of miniature locomotives. From N to OO and even potentially lesser-known scales like TT (Tri-ang) and ScaleSeven. However, have you heard of something called L Gauge? This is the scale that collectors of LEGO Trains use to refer to their area of interest and, although it may not be an officially recognised scale, it's an increasingly popular and interesting variation on traditional model railways. Here we'll look at the history of L Gauge and some of the sets produced by LEGO.

But first it's worth exploring the history of LEGO a little to see where it all began. Although the LEGO Group was first formed way back in 1932 it wasn't until 1949 that the company began producing those famous little plastic bricks. Originally called 'Automatic Binding Bricks' the blocks were based on a design by a company called Kiddicraft. The initial blocks were simple affairs that lacked versatility and in 1958 they were redesigned slightly into the shape we see today. They've remained almost the same ever since and modern bricks released today still slot together with those made in 1958.

In 1965 LEGO ventured into the world of railway with the release of the imaginatively titled 323 Train – although it had no track and ran on ordinary wheels. Resembling an American steam loco, the model was made from a mix of mainly red bricks with white/blue detailing and a grey roof. The 323 only lasted a year and was quickly replaced by model 080, which came with a simple blue and white track along with a small village of four houses

Modern LEGO sets include a number of different accessories and figures, as shown here with the 7937 Train Station set... or should that really be Railway Station?

to give some colour to a layout. However, it didn't have a motor, so required 'people power' to get the wheels moving. Being one of the earlier examples means that 323 can trade for a couple of hundred quid, when it's in good condition.

However, 1966 really saw LEGO entering into the model railway market, with the release of set 115, which had a 4.5v motor to move the loco. This new kit came with a blue power pack and large black motor that was placed inside the locomotive. The wheels were further developed and now came flanged with rubber rims

for traction. Although not as nice to look at as its predecessors, the 115 still included the blue/white tracks and three simple wagons to tow along – initially the wagons could only be hooked on but in later sets the hooks were replaced by magnets.

In the early days of L gauge, users were fairly limited by the products available, although extra track, including points and crossovers were available. In 1969 LEGO also released a 12v version (no. 720) with a metal rail system feeding electricity to the engine, rather than a battery with an ugly wire on. The initial

4.5v and 12v trains were released between 1966 until 1979 – a period which is called the 'blue era' because of the blue track used.

After the blue era came the grey era, which is more exciting than it sounds. Between 1980 and 1990 LEGO made new model railway sets with dark grey sleepers and light grey rails, while the wheels were red or black. Arguably this was the golden era for collectors, as LEGO released a huge selection of accessories and locomotives. Some of the more sophisticated locos even featured working lights for the front and rear but, more importantly, the wheels

DIECAST RAILWAYS TOY FIGURES TINPLATE TV & FILM OTHERS EBUYS

ABOVE
Emerald Night, seen here, heralded the latest developments in the L gauge range and was launched in 1999.

ABOVE RIGHT
One of the recent LEGO Trains is this, the Horizon Express, which retails for £79.99. It features more than 1,300 blocks.

RIGHT
Although colourful, some of the earlier LEGO Trains sets didn't look particularly realistic... although we would love to see this speeding through Clapham Junction.

BELOW
Another recent addition to the range, the LEGO Passenger Train, uses new flexible tracks, along with a four-channel, seven-speed infrared remote control, which can run up to eight different trains at once - perfect for those with a large layout featuring numerous different trains.

Early LEGO sets are sought after by L gauge collectors.

ABOVE
In the late '90s LEGO Trains officially became part of the City range, so you can run them alongside your various emergency vehicles, offices, shops and other buildings, which are also in the ever-growing City series.

now tilted, which allowed for tighter turns and more realistic movement.

In terms of accessories, enthusiasts were certainly spoilt for choice with a great variety of items – many of which LEGO has never produced again. These included remote controlled points, remote controlled signals, automatic uncouplers, working station lights, flashing lights, a level crossing with automatic barriers and lots more. Compared to the basic sets of the late '60s, the grey era was a revolution and is probably the closest the LEGO Trains have got to being just like standard model railways.

One of the more impressive LEGO trains released during this period was no. 7740 the Inter-City Passenger Train Set. Sold from 1980 and featuring more than 780 LEGO bricks it was one of the few grey era sets that could carry passengers and 10 Minifigures were included. You could even expand the impressive train with the addition of the Postal Container Wagon (7819) and Passenger Carriage/Sleeper (7815) to create a truly standout model.

In 1991 it was all change, as LEGO scrapped the 4.5v and 12v ranges and replaced them with a new 9v system. Tracks changed again, with power now being transmitted directly through metal strips on the two running rails. This meant previous 12v releases were no longer compatible without modification and LEGO reduced the amount of accessories with no remote control functions or automatic signaling products. Despite all this, the actual design of the trains did improve, like the futuristic-looking Railway Express (4561) with vehicle carrier and passenger car that has a movie screen/seats.

The 9v system lasted for 16 years before it was scrapped for a new line of remote-controlled trains with all-plastic track (to save on costs). However, the RC Trains range only lasted for two years before LEGO launched Power Functions (PF) Trains with the release of a new train called Emerald Night, as part of the LEGO City series. The benefit of the Power Functions Train is that they're compatible with other powered sets from LEGO, such as vehicles and even dinosaurs – ensuring there's plenty of scope for interesting tracks. So the future certainly looks bright for L gauge enthusiasts. ■

Trix Twin Railway 4-6-2 tender engine 'Brittania' 70000, good overall condiiton but dusty, with good box. Sold for £100, Aston's, September.

Hornby Metropolitan locomotive fitted with LV motor, finished in red with yellow lining, some chips on paintwork. Fair condition. Sold for £230, Hartleys, September.

Hornby O Gauge 6-volt LMS 2270 0-4-0T Locomotive, good condition. Sold for £70, Warwick & Warwick, September.

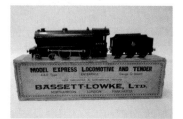

Bassett-Lowke 4-4-0 Enterprise locomotive and tender, spirit fired, finished in green with '62759' to cab. Scorching to boiler, some paint damage, boxed. Fair condition. Sold for £280, Hartleys, September.

Hornby O Gauge clockwork LNER green 623 No. 1 0-4-0T Locomotive, generally good with key in working order, minor re-touching in fair box. Sold for £55, Warwick & Warwick, September.

Bassett-Lowke by Bing 1921 series GWR 8271 First Class Coach No. 65/0, good plus in fair box, tape to edges of lid. Sold for £200, Warwick & Warwick, September.

Trix OO gauge Warship class D801 'Vanguard', good in good box. Sold for £30, Aston's, September.

Hornby O Gauge clockwork LMS maroon 8712 No. 1 Special 0-4-0 Locomotive and Tender, generally good, minor repairs, with key in working order. Sold for £70, Warwick & Warwick, September.

Hornby Dublo BR Mk1 Restaurant Car (RU) BR E1939 maroon No. 4971, excellent plus in excellent box. Sold for £65, Warwick & Warwick, September.

Trix OO Gauge BR green 'Scotsman' and Tender, good to very good condition. Sold for £110, Special Auction Services, December.

Hornby O Gauge No. 2 locomotive and tender 4-4-0 LMS 2711, missing R/H rear step, a few dents and scratches. No key. Passable to fair condition in passable box. Sold for £480, Aston's, October.

Hornby Dublo 3R 3226 BR maroon 4-6-2 'City of Liverpool', has been refitted, good in a fair plus box. Sold for £220, Cottees, September.

Hornby O Gauge No. 3 4-4-2 LMS maroon clockwork locomotive 'Royal Scot 6100', very good, unboxed. Sold for £120, Aston's, October.

Hornby Dublo 2R 2233 CO BO Diesel Electric No. D5702, missing a coupling, otherwise excellent. Boxed. Sold for £40, Cottees, September.

Hornby O Gauge No. 3 E320 4-4-2 LNER green 20v electric locomotive 'Flying Scotsman 4472' with headlight, very good, some paint damage to front of tender, repairing to front buffer beam, unboxed. Sold for £160, Aston's, October.

Graham Farish OO BR blue MN 4-6-2 'Belgian Marine', an excellent plus working example with no sign of body or wheel fatigue in a good original box. Sold for £190, Cottees, September.

DIECAST   RAILWAYS   TOY FIGURES   TINPLATE   TV & FILM   OTHERS   EBUYS

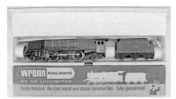

Wrenn Railways LMS 'Duchess' 8P Class 4-6-2 BR 46242 'City of Glasgow' blue No. W2229, excellent plus in excellent box, with packing pieces. Sold for £70, Warwick & Warwick, September.

Wrenn Railways OO Gauge locomotive W2225A 2-8-0 LMS freight, very good in good box. Sold for £60, Aston's, October.

Graham Farish OO Southern green Battle of Britain 4-6-2 'Sir Eustace Missenden' in Golden Arrow livery, early motor shows signs of life but needs service, otherwise an excellent example. Sold for £160, Cottees, September.

Wrenn Railways 'Duchess' 8P Class 4-6-2 BR 46235 'City of Birmingham' green No. W2228, about mint in excellent box with packing pieces and instructions. Sold for £75, Warwick & Warwick, September.

Trix OO 1050 BR green Class A4 4-6-2 'Merlin', excellent in a blue collectors box. Sold for £30, Cottees, September.

Wrenn Railways Class A4 4-6-2 60014 'Silver Link' green No. W2211, about mint in excellent box with packing pieces. Sold for £120, Warwick & Warwick, September.

Hornby Minitrix N 214 LNER A4 4-6-2 blue 'Sir Nigel Gresley' No. 4498, excellent plus, boxed with instructions. Sold for £40, Cottees, September.

Wrenn Railways Class A4 4-6-2 NE 4903 'Peregrine' wartime black No. W2213, about mint in excellent box with packing pieces and instructions. Sold for £85, Warwick & Warwick, September.

Hornby Minitrix 12950 LNER green A2 4-6-2 'Flying Scotsman', excellent plus, boxed with instructions. Sold for £40, Cottees, September.

Trix Express HO Gauge 3-rail 'Alder' 2-2-2 locomotive, with three four-wheel coaches. Good with fair outer box, internal packing missing. Sold for £40, Aston's, October.

Wrenn Railways BR 4MT Standard Tank 2-6-4T Southern 1927 green No. W2245 lined, excellent in good plus box. Sold for £48, Warwick & Warwick, September.

Wrenn Railways OO Gauge locomotive W2238 4-6-2 'Clanline' BR green, very good in good box. Sold for £90, Aston's, October.

Wrenn Railways OO Gauge locomotive W2237 4-6-2 West Country Southern 'Lyme Regis', very good in good box. Sold for £75, Aston's, October.

Hornby Dublo 2-Rail No. 2235 4-6-2 SR West Country Class 'Barnstaple' 34005, very good in good box, with slight fading. Sold for £75, Aston's, October.

Bachmann Branchline OO Gauge 31-177DS ''Kolhapur'' 4-6-0 Jubilee Class locomotive and six wheel tender, BR green livery with early emblem, No.6P45593, window boxed with inner vacuform plastic display piece and outer cardboard sleeve. Sold for £100, Bamfords, October.

Hornby O Gauge No. 1 Special 0-4-0T GWR (button) green clockwork locomotive '5500', very good with slight damage to decal and small chips to paint, unboxed. Sold for £95, Aston's, September.

Bachmann Branchline OO Gauge 32-002 'Saint Edmund Hall' 4-6-0 Hall Class locomotive and six wheel tender, BR black livery with early emblem, No.5960, window boxed, literature and illustrated cardboard sleeve piece. Sold for £45, Bamfords, October.

Hornby O Gauge No. 3 E320 4-4-2 GWR green 20v electric locomotive 'Caerphilly Castle' 4097, button logo on No. 2 tender, headlight. Very good with some minor chips to paint, unboxed. Sold for £200, Aston's, September.

Wrenn Railways OO Gauge W2209 'Golden Eagle' 4-6-2 Class A4 locomotive and eight wheel tender, LNER green livery, No.4482, boxed with three inner cardboard packaging rings. Sold for £85, Bamfords, October.

Hornby Dublo 2-rail 2030 Diesel Electric Goods Set, included is a Meccano order form and Hornby Dublo instructions, also contains track, excellent, box good. Sold for £100, Vectis, September.

Hornby O Gauge 'Zulu' 0-4-0 black clockwork locomotive, splasher decals 'Zulu' in red/gold to left, 'Meccano Limited Liverpool' in red/gold, 'MLdL' logo on tender. Very good condition, unboxed. Sold for £110, Aston's, September.

Wrenn Railways OO Gauge W2217 0-6-2 tank locomotive, LNER green livery, No.9522, boxed with two inner cardboard packaging rings and literature. Sold for £30, Bamfords, October.

Hornby O Gauge original advertising board, made 1930s, depicting 4-4-2 6100 Royal Scot with Pullman coaches. Fold out stands to rear. Small tear to the front and slightly dog-eared in places. Sold for £150, Aston's, September.

Hornby O Gauge No. 1 Special 0-4-0T LMS (sans-serif) maroon 20v locomotive '70', very good condition. Sold for £110, Aston's, September.

Hornby Dublo 2-rail 2009 0-6-0 Tank Passenger Train BR containing BR black R1 Tank Locomotive No.31337, with a circle of track, an order form for Meccano, a Hornby Dublo guarantee, generally excellent, box good plus. Sold for £80, Vectis, September.

Hornby Dublo 2-rail 2220 4-6-0 BR Castle Class Locomotive 'Denbigh Castle' No.7032, in green complete with instruction booklet dated 8/859/40 and a purple guarantee slip and a yellow tested tag, condition is excellent, box good plus in plain red. Sold for £90, Vectis, September.

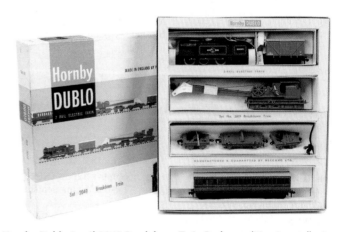

Hornby Dublo 2-rail 2049 Breakdown Train Pack, condition is excellent, also included is some lubricating oil and a tested tag, box good plus. Sold for £260, Vectis, September.

Hornby Dublo 2-rail 2231 0-6-0 BR Diesel Shunter No.D3302, in green in original red striped box, general condition is good, box good. Sold for £35, Vectis, September.

Hornby Dublo 2-rail 2245 3300BHP Electric Locomotive Bo-Bo BR E3002, in blue with Lion & Crown BR logo to side, generally excellent, box good plus with a reproduction insert, slight rust to one of the pantographs. Sold for £320, Vectis, September.

Hornby O Gauge No. 2 Special E220 4-4-0 LMS maroon 'Compund' 20v electric locomotive '1185', very good but paint loss to front buffer beam, front bogie wheels have been replaced, unboxed. Sold for £240, Aston's, September.

Hornby O Gauge Private Owner Van 'Jacob & Co's Biscuits', maroon with T3 black chassis, moderate chipping to roof, otherwise very good, unboxed. Sold for £50, Aston's, September.

Hornby Dublo OO Gauge 3-rail (32049) D1 Caboose, Canadian Pacific Railway (CPR) black body, No.437270, boxed - dark blue box with patent label. Sold for £200, Bamfords, October.

Wrenn Railways OO Gauge No.2226 'City of London' 4-6-2 locomotive and six wheel tender, BR maroon livery, No.8 46245, boxed with one inner cardboard packaging ring and literature. Sold for £55, Bamfords, October.

Hornby O Gauge No. 2 4-4-4T LMS maroon clockwork locomotive '2107', very good with some paint damage to keyhole area with good box. Sold for £120, Aston's, September.

Wrenn Railways OO Gauge W2226/A 'City of Carlisle' 4-6-2 locomotive and six wheel tender, BR maroon livery, No.8 46238, boxed with two inner cardboard packaging rings and literature. Sold for £150, Bamfords, October.

Hornby Dublo 2-rail 2233 Co-Bo Diesel Electric Locomotive BR D5702, in green, near mint with original card protectors still sprung to body in good plus box with instructions and purple guarantee slip, also has yellow tested tag. Sold for £180, Vectis, September.

Wrenn Railways OO Gauge W2228/A 'City of Edinburgh' 4-6-2 locomotive and six wheel tender, BR green livery, No.8 46241, boxed with two inner cardboard packaging rings and literature. Sold for £170, Bamfords, October.

Wrenn Railways OO Gauge W2229/A 'City of Manchester' 4-6-2 locomotive and six wheel tender, BR blue livery, No.8 46246, boxed with one inner cardboard packaging ring and literature. Sold for £160, Bamfords, October.

Hornby O Gauge original advertising board, made in 1930s, depicting 4-4-0 LNER 234 'Yorkshire' with Pullman coaches. Repaired fold out stand to rear. Small crease to the front right and slightly dog-eared. Sold for £130, Aston's, September.

Wrenn Railways OO Gauge W2241 'Duchess of Hamilton' 4-6-2- locomotive and six wheel tender, LMS black livery, No.7P 6229, boxed with two inner packaging rings and literature. Sold for £85, Bamfords, October.

Wrenn Railways OO Gauge W2246 2-6-4 Caledonian Railway tank locomotive, CR blue livery, No.2085, boxed with two inner cardboard packaging rings and literature. Sold for £95, Bamfords, October.

Trix Trains OO Gauge 'Merlin' 4-6-2 locomotive and eight wheel tender, BR green livery, No.60027, window boxed with inner vacuform plastic display piece and instructions sheet. Sold for £30, Bamfords, October.

Hornby Dublo 2-Rail Train Set No. 2049 'Breakdown Train', contains 0-6-2 BR black locomotive No. 69550, maroon coach and breakdown crane. Very good to excellent in good box. Damage to lid corners and slightly grubby. Sold for £160, Aston's, September.

Trix Trains OO Gauge 2-rail 4-6-0 Class A4 4468 'Mallard' in garter blue, very good in fair box. Sold for £40, Aston's, September.

Hornby Dublo OO Gauge 3226 'City of Liverpool' LMR 4-6-2 locomotive and six wheel, tender BR maroon livery, No.8 46247, boxed with inner yellow cardboard packaging piece and two cardboard packaging rings (some tape to box lid). Sold for £220, Bamfords, October.

Trix Twin Railway 'Meteor' Diesel Express Articulated 3-car diesel train, good overall, some paint loss to each end, rusting at handrails, with fair to good box. Sold for £100, Aston's, September.

Hornby Dublo 2-Rail Train Set No. 2034 'The Royal Scot', contains Diesel Deltic locomotive D9012 'Crepello', two maroon coaches and track. Very good in good box - missing one end to lid. Sold for £100, Aston's, September.

Hornby Railways OO Gauge R2433 Eddie Stobart 'Daniel Appleby' Class 47 Co-Co diesel electric locomotive, green livery, No.47 900, No.0363 of a limited production run of 1,000, window boxed with display piece, certificate of authenticity, illustrated cardboard sleeve piece and illustrated outer cardboard sleeve piece. Sold for £50, Bamfords, October.

Hornby 1939-41 LMS Breakdown Van and Crane, black base and bogies with grey body and jib lined dark grey, white roof, small gold serif LMS both sides, sliding side doors, chips to roof otherwise good to very good. Sold for £30, Lacy, Scott & Knight, November.

Wrenn W2241 Duchess of Hamilton LMS 6229, black, with instructions, excellent, box good to excellent, stamped 'Packer No. 3'. Sold for £100, Tennants, December.

Hornby Dublo EDLT20 3R BR Green 4-6-0 Bristol Castle 7013 locomotive and tender, boxed, with instructions. Sold for £60, Reeman Dansie, December.

Tri-ang Railways 00 Gauge RS29 Holiday Express Train Set, BR black 4-6-0 B12 and two BR blood and custard coaches and track, in original set box with card protector, very good to excellent, box very good. Sold for £55, Special Auction Services, December.

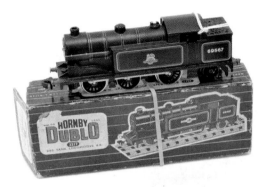

Hornby Dublo 3-Rail 3217 0-6-2T BR 69567 Locomotive, coal in bunker, plastic rear wheels, excellent, box fair to good, torn. Sold for £140, Tennants, December.

Hornby Dublo 00 Gauge 2-Rail 2033 Co-Bo Diesel-Electric Goods Train Set, comprising Co-Bo D5702 Diesel Locomotive, four wagons, oval of track, oil, rail clips and literature, in original late blue and white picture box, excellent, box very good. Sold for £210, Special Auction Services, December.

An uncommon Hornby Dublo 00 Gauge 3-Rail EDG7 SR Goods Train Set, comprising olive green 0-6-2T 2594, three trucks, track, Instructions and transformer, in original set box with Royal Scot picture label, circa 1947, good. Loco with small area of paint loss, corrosion due to damp storage, box good. Sold for £750, Special Auction Services, December.

Hornby Dublo 00 Gauge D1 Post-War 2-Coach Articulated Unit, comprising two coaches, in original light blue box, with repair label and dated 5/48, good, replacement Hornby/Peco style long reach couplings fitted to each end, box very good. Sold for £360, Special Auction Services, December.

Hornby Dublo 00 Gauge 2-Rail 2035 Pullman Train SR 'Luxury Set of the Year' Train Set, comprising West Country Class 'Barnstaple', three Pullman Coaches, oval of track, oil, literature, Headboard and Nameboards for 'Bournemouth Belle' and Rail Clips, in original blue and yellow Set box with gold 'Luxury Set of the Year' sash, excellent, box very good. Sold for £150, Special Auction Services, December.

Trix Twin 4-6-2 Loco and Tender BR green "Scotsman" No.60103, good to good plus in good box. Sold for £120, Vectis, December.

Bassett-Lowke Winteringham Private Owner Open Wagon, good condition. Sold for £80, Lacy, Scott & Knight, November.

Wrenn W2209 Golden Eagle LNER 4482, green with instructions, excellent, stamped 'Packer No. 6'. Sold for £90, Tennants, December.

Wrenn W2237Lyme Regis Southern 21C109, green with instructions, excellent, box good to excellent. Sold for £100, Tennants, December.

Wrenn 00 Gauge W2301 Coronation Class 'Queen Elizabeth', in blue, in original box, excellent, box very good. Sold for £550, Special Auction Services, December.

Hornby Dublo 00 Gauge 3-Rail 3224 2-8-0 8F Locomotive and Tender, in BR black No 48158, in original blue striped picture box, excellent, box fair to good, ink writing on lid. Sold for £90, Special Auction Services, December.

Hornby Dublo 00 Gauge 2-Rail converted to 3-Rail 2245 E3002 Electric Locomotive, in BR blue, good quality conversion, appears to be using original Dublo pick ups and may have been factory fitted, instructions dated 9/63, in original yellow and red striped picture box, very good to excellent, box very good. Sold for £380, Special Auction Services, December.

Hornby Dublo 00 Gauge 3-Rail 3232 Co-Co Diesel Electric Locomotive, in BR green, both with instructions, guarantee 1/60, Train Instructions and Tested Tag, in original blue striped picture box, very good to excellent, box good to very good. Sold for £75, Special Auction Services, December.

Wrenn 00 Gauge W2291 West Country Class 'Sidmouth', in BR green, in original box, excellent, box very good. Sold for £400, Special Auction Services, December.

Hornby Dublo OO Gauge late 3-Rail 3235 'Dorchester', in BR green, in original box, good, some chips to lining mainly under cab windows, box poor to fair, wear on edges, all lid corners loose, lacks one end of lid. Sold for £180, Special Auction Services, December.

Hornby O Gauge No. 3C Clockwork 4-4-2 Royal Scot 6100 with LMS Tender, good to good plus, with replacement mechanism and wheels. Sold for £120, Warwick & Warwick, November.

Trix OO Gauge LMS crimson lake 6201 'Princess' and Tender, good to very good, some paint chips, mazac blister on the offside pony frame. Sold for £230, Special Auction Services, December.

Trix OO Gauge BR blue 60103 'Scotsman' and Tender, good, some paint loss to tender. Sold for £180, Special Auction Services, December.

Wrenn 00 Gauge W221A Bristol Castle, in BR green, in original box, excellent, box very good. Sold for £200, Special Auction Services, December.

Wrenn W4652P Auto Distributors Limited Lowmac Wagon, with red Ford Anglia and yellow Caravan. Near mint to mint in excellent to near mint Tri-ang/Wrenn box. Sold for £90, Vectis, December.

Hornby Dublo 00 Gauge 3-Rail 3234 Co-Co Diesel Electric Locomotive 'St Paddy', in BR two tone green, instructions for 3232, yellow tested tag, oil and spanner, in original yellow and blue striped picture box, very good, box very good. Sold for £290, Special Auction Services, December.

Hornby 1940-41 Esso Petrol Tank Wagon, in buff box, very good, box good. Sold for £80, Lacy, Scott & Knight, November.

Hornby O Gauge E320 20v 4-4-2 Caerphilly Castle 4073 Locomotive and GWR Tender, in good plus condition, some small chips to raised edges. Sold for £190, Warwick & Warwick, November.

Hornby Dublo OO Gauge 3-Rail EDL17 LNER green 0-6-2T, in original plain mid blue box, excellent, box very good. Sold for £150, Special Auction Services, December.

Hornby Dublo 00 Gauge 2-Rail 2220 BR green 'Denbigh Castle', in original plain red box, excellent, box good. Sold for £210, Special Auction Services, December.

Hornby Dublo 00 Gauge 2-Rail 2234 BR two tone green Deltic Diesel Electric Locomotive 'Crepello', in original red striped box, excellent, box fair, two lid corners loose. Sold for £85, Special Auction Services, December.

Hornby Dublo 00 Gauge 2-Rail 2211 BR green A4 'Golden Fleece' Locomotive and Tender, in original red striped box, excellent, box good to very good. Sold for £130, Special Auction Services, December.

Hornby Dublo OO Gauge 2-Rail 2218 BR black 2-6-4T, in original red striped box, excellent, box very good. Sold for £130, Special Auction Services, December.

Hornby O Gauge Electrical Viaduct, in three pieces, good plus in fair box. Sold for £47, Warwick & Warwick, November.

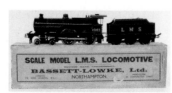

Bassett-Lowke 5302/0 LMS Standard Compound 4-4-0 locomotive, maroon 1063 with tender, 12v DC with instruction booklet and box for clockwork model. Very good, box fair to good. Sold for £370, Lacy, Scott & Knight, November.

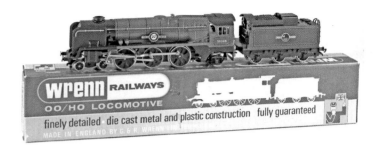

Wrenn Railways BR Green 35028 Clan Line Merchant Navy Class 4-6-2 Locomotive and Tender No. W2238, about mint in excellent box, stamped 'Packer No. 6'. Sold for £65, Warwick & Warwick, May.

Hornby Dublo OO Gauge 3-Rail 'City of Liverpool' Locomotive, BR maroon No. 46247, in original box, good to very good, box passable to fair. Sold for £290, Special Auction Services, April.

Tri-ang Railways OO Gauge RS70 clockwork Train Set, containing Tank Locomotive 0-4-0 in plain black, together with Open Top Coach in maroon and Closed Top Coach in light blue, comes with clockwork key and a small quantity of track, general condition is excellent, box good to good plus. Sold for £35, Vectis, April.

Hornby Dublo GWR Green 6699 Class N2 0-6-2T Locomotive No. EDL7, excellent in good box with correct GW sticker on end. Sold for £180, Warwick & Warwick, May.

Bassett-Lowke 3-Rail Electric 4-4-0 LMS 1108 Compound Locomotive, maroon, good, some damage mainly to tender, box poor to fair. Sold for £160, Tennants, December.

Hornby 1930-36 Maroon LMS Clockwork No. 2 Special Tank Locomotive 4-4-2 No. 2180, missing two cab hand rails, some small chips and scratches, good, box passable. Sold for £160, Lacy, Scott & Knight, November.

Wrenn W5100 Ventilated Van 'Wrenn Railways', near mint to mint in near mint box. Sold for £40, Vectis, December.

Wrenn 00 Gauge W2306 BR green A4 4-6-2 'Dominion of Canada', No. 60010, fitted with large size driving wheels, instructions, in original box stamped Packer No. 2 90314, excellent, box very good. Sold for £550, Special Auction Services, December.

Wrenn 00 Gauge W2241 AM2 5 Pole Motor LMS black 4-6-2 'Duchess of Gloucester', No. 6225, instructions, in original box stamped Packer No. 3, excellent, box very good. Sold for £400, Special Auction Services, December.

Bing Black-lined Red L&NWR Clockwork 'Precurser' 4-4-2 Tank Locomotive No. 44, paintwork crazed, wear around keyhole. Fair to good. Sold for £170, Lacy, Scott & Knight, November.

Hornby 1938-41 Maroon LMS Compound Clockwork No. 2 Special 4-4-0 Locomotive No. 1185, small chips to steam dome and firebox, with six-wheel LMS tender, both very good. Sold for £300, Lacy, Scott & Knight, November.

Hornby 1929-30 Green Clockwork No. 2 Special Locomotive 'County of Bedford' No. 3821, some touching in, front buffer beam repainted and coupling broken, with six-wheel 'Great Western' tender, fair to good. Sold for £260, Lacy, Scott & Knight, November.

Carette for Bassett-Lowke GII MR 30 Ton Bogie Coal Wagon, very good, box fair. Sold for £200, Lacy, Scott & Knight, November.

Hornby Dublo 00 Gauge 3-Rail EDL17 BR gloss black 0-6-2T, No. 69567, in original plain mid blue box, excellent, box very good. Sold for £65, Special Auction Services, December.

Hornby 1926 GW Snowplough, on black open axelguard base, GW on base, grey body, red-lined plough, 'Snow Plough' on grey enamelled doors, small chips to lining and roof, otherwise good to very good. Sold for £100, Lacy, Scott &Knight, November.

Hornby 1936-39 Colas Bitumen Tank Wagon, on lighter blue standard base with red tank, some small chips to tank, two stays replaced. Sold for £180, Lacy, Scott & Knight, November.

A Hornby Dublo 00 Gauge 4685 Caustic Liquor Bogle Wagon, plate bogies, in ICI blue, in original red striped box, excellent, box very good. Sold for £60, Special Auction Services, December.

Hornby Dublo 00 Gauge 2001 Ready-to-run Train Set, three trucks, transformer and circle of track, in original box with picture sleeve, polystyrene insert in red inner box, very good, box good to very good, tear to lid. Sold for £140, Special Auction Services, December.

Hornby 1939-41 Mobiloil Oil Tank Wagon, very good to near mint, box good. Sold for £65, Lacy, Scott & Knight, November.

Hornby 1939-41 Redline-Gilco Petrol Tank Wagon, very good to near mint, box good. Sold for £75, Lacy, Scott & Knight, November.

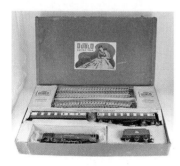

Hornby Dublo Passenger Train Set No. EDP12, with BR gloss green 46232 Duchess of Montrose 4-6-2 locomotive and tender, two coaches and track, generally good in nearly good repaired box. Sold for £32, Warwick & Warwick, November.

An uncommon Hornby Dublo 00 Gauge 2-Rail 4685 Caustic Liquor Bogie Wagon, with diamond bogies, in ICI blue, in original red striped box, excellent, box very good. Sold for £190, Special Auction Services, December.

Hornby Dublo 3-rail EDP3 Passenger Train Set, containing CPR 4-6-2 1215 in black livery with an oval of track in original box with instructions, general condition good plus, box fair. Sold for £240, Vectis, March.

Tri-ang Railways OO Gauge Electric Set R1, containing Steam Locomotive 4-6-2 class 8P "Princess Victoria" No.46205 in BR black livery, together with two Passenger Coaches in maroon and cream and a small quantity of track with instructions and original corrugated card, good plus, box is good. Sold for £30, Vectis, April.

Hornby Dublo BR Green 34042 Dorchester Locomotive and Tender No. 3235, excellent in excellent box with Beatties sticker. Sold for £220, Warwick & Warwick, May.

Wrenn W2223 4-6-0 Loco and Tender Cattle Class BR Blue "Windsor Castle" No.4082, excellent to excellent plus in good plus box. Includes instructions. Sold for £90, Vectis, March.

Wrenn W2228 M2 4-6-2 Loco and Tender Duchess Class BR Green "City of Birmingham" No.46235, excellent to near mint in good box, base coded 00233. Includes instructions. Sold for £150, Vectis, March.

Hornby Dublo BR 34041 Dorchester Rebuilt 'West Country' Class No. 3235, good plus in good plus box, small chip to cab roof, some minor paint loss to raised edges. Sold for £150, Warwick & Warwick, May.

Hornby Dublo 3-rail LT25 Freight Locomotive and Tender of a Class 8F 2-8-0 No.48158, in BR black in blue striped box, general condition is good plus, box good. Sold for £70, Vectis, March.

Trix Twin 3-rail F105B EM1 Bo-Bo BR Lined Black Overhead Electric Locomotive No. 26010, excellent in good box. Sold for £90, Vectis, March.

Hornby Dublo BR Green 7032 Denbigh Castle 4-6-0 Locomotive and Tender No. 2220, excellent in good plain red box. Sold for £50, Warwick & Warwick, March.

Hornby Dublo LNER Green 9596 Class N2 0-6-2T Locomotive No. EDL7, excellent in good plus box. Sold for £85, Warwick & Warwick, May.

Hornby Dublo BR Green 60030 Golden Fleece Locomotive and Tender No. 2211, excellent plus in good box with instructions, repair sticker to one end. Sold for £70, Warwick & Warwick, May.

Hornby Dublo BR Bown and Cream W1910 Restaurant Car No. 4070, excellent plus in nearly excellent box. Sold for £60, Warwick & Warwick, March.

Hornby Dublo 2-rail 4076 6-wheeled Passenger Brake Van excellent in excellent box. Sold for £70, Vectis, June.

Hornby Dublo 3-rail LT25 2-8-0 Engine and Tender minor blemishes to raised edges, some graffiti to box lid. Good, box good. Sold for £85, Lacy, Scott & Knight, May.

Hornby Dublo 2-rail 2220 4-6-0 locomotive and tender Castle Class BR green 'Denbigh Castle' No. 7032 excellent in good plus plain red box, test certificate, guarantee slip and instructions. Sold for £100, Vectis, June.

Hornby Dublo 3-rail L30 Bo-Bo Diesel Locomotive would benefit from cleaning otherwise good. Sold for £60, Lacy, Scott & Knight, May.

Hornby Dublo 3-rail Co-Bo Diesel Locomotive with guarantee, pencil mark on box, very good, box good. Sold for £100, Lacy, Scott & Knight, May.

Wrenn Railways Brighton Belle 2-car set W3006/7 in brown/cream livery, in box with instructions, excellent. Sold for £160, Special Auction Services, July.

Hornby Dublo BR Green 7032 Denbigh Castle 4-6-0 Locomotive and Tender No. 2220, excellent in good plain red box. Sold for £50, Warwick & Warwick, March.

Wrenn Railways W2232 BR blue 0-6-0 diesel shunter, packer No. 3 on box base, mint, box good. Sold for £40, Lacy, Scott & Knight, August.

Wrenn Railways W2220 GWR green 2-6-4 tank engine, vacuum pipe added to front and buffer beam. Good, box good. Sold for £50, Lacy, Scott & Knight, August.

Wrenn Railways W2274 5-pole motor 4-6-0 locomotive and tender LMS maroon Royal Scott Class 'Lancashire Witch' No. 6125, near mint to mint in near mint box. Sold for £420, Vectis, June.

Wrenn Railways Goods Wagon W5100A Ventilated Van 'Wrenn Railways', near mint in near mint box. Sold for £100, Vectis, June.

Wrenn Railways W2265/A Bulleid Pacific 'Fighter Pilot', SR malachite green with Golden Arrow insignia, near mint, box near mint. Sold for £210, Lacy, Scott & Knight, August.

Trix Trains LNER Grey 'Silver Link' Engine and Tender, Tri-ang coupling fitted, good, box good. Sold for £50, Lacy, Scott & Knight, May.

Wrenn Railways W2302 Coronation Class locomotive and tender 'King George VI', in LMS red, original box stamped 'Packer No. 3 04518', excellent. Sold for £440, Special Auction Services, July.

Bassett-Lowke O Gauge Electric 4-6-0 Locomotive No. 6100 'Royal Scot' and Tender, finished in LMS maroon livery (some playwear and paint splashes to tender). Sold for £320, Toovey's, March.

Bassett-Lowke O Gauge Clockwork 4-4-0 Compound Locomotive No. 1108 and Tender, finished in LMS maroon livrey with yellow and black lining (some paint damage, tender coupling link replaced). Sold for £150, Toovey's, March.

Bassett-Lowke O Gauge Clockwork 2-6-0 Mogul Locomotive No. 1300 and Tender, finished in Midland maroon livery (some repairs and re-touching, boiler slightly dented). Sold for £180, Toovey's, March.

Bing Gauge O Clockwork 4-4-0 Compound Locomotive No. 999 and Tender, finished in Midland maroon livery with yellow and black lining (some faults, reverse pick-up removed). Sold for £180, Toovey's, March.

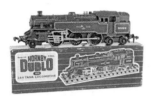

Hornby Dublo BR 80059 Class 4MT Standard Tank No. 3218 good plus in good plus box. Sold for £180, Warwick & Warwick, May.

Hornby Dublo D9001 St. Paddy 'Deltic' Type (Class 55) Diesel Co-Co Locomotive No. 3234, good to good plus in good plus box, some paint loss to raised edges. Sold for £160, Warwick & Warwick, May.

Hornby Dublo OO Gauge 3-Rail 3250 BR SR green EMU Driving Car, good, lacks one set of sideframes, a little grubby and one couple down bar broken. Sold for £110, Special Auction Services, April.

Hornby Dublo 3-rail LT25 Freight Locomotive and Tender Class 8F 2-8-0 No.48158, in BR black livery in blue striped box, generally excellent, box good plus. Sold for £110, Vectis, March.

Hornby Dublo 2-rail Locomotive and Tender of a 2-8-0 Class 8F No.48109, in BR black livery with instructions and guarantee slip in plain red box with label to one end, condition is excellent, box good plus. Sold for £110, Vectis, March.

Hornby Dublo 2-rail 2217 Tank Locomotive of an 0-6-2 Class N2 No.69550, in BR black, general condition is fair to good, box good. Sold for £40, Vectis, March.

Hornby Dublo 3-rail 3221 Locomotive and Tender of a 4-6-0 "Ludlow Castle" No.5002, in BR green livery in blue striped box, generally excellent, box good to good plus. Sold for £260, Vectis, March.

Hornby Dublo 2-rail 2233 Co-Bo Diesel Electric Locomotive No.D5702, in BR green livery in original box, general condition is good plus, box good slightly faded. Sold for £70, Vectis, March.

Hornby Dublo 2-rail 2250 Electric Motor Coach Brake 2nd BR(S) No.S65326, in green, generally excellent, box good plus. Sold for £100, Vectis, March.

Hornby Dublo 2-rail 2235 Locomotive and Tender West Country Class Locomotive Barnstaple No.34005, in BR green livery, comes with guarantee slip and instructions in a red striped box, generally good plus, box good. Sold for £110, Vectis, March.

Hornby Dublo 3-rail 3211 Locomotive and Tender of 4-6-2 "Mallard" No.60022, in BR green livery, locomotive pony and rear wheels are plastic contained in original blue striped box, generally good plus, box good. Sold for £120, Vectis, March.

Hornby Dublo 2-rail 2232 Co-Co Diesel Electric Locomotive, in BR green, comes with guarantee slip and instructions in original box, generally excellent, box good plus. Sold for £70, Vectis, March.

Wrenn OO Gauge W2304 'City of Leeds', in BR maroon, with alternative of King George VI nameplate and instructions, in original box titled Leeds/King George VI and stamped 2 91 729, very good to excellent. Sold for £350, Special Auction Services, April.

Hornby Dublo 3-rail 3226 'City of Liverpool' Engine and Tender, with instructions, minor touching in to boiler. Good, box good. Sold for £220, Lacy, Scott & Knight, May.

Wrenn Railways BR maroon 'City of London' engine and tender, a few minor blemishes, good condition. Sold for £50, Lacy, Scott & Knight, August.

Trix Trains LNER Blue 'Mallard' Engine and Tender, Tri-ang coupling fitted, good, box good. Sold for £50, Lacy, Scott & Knight, May.

Hornby Dublo 3-rail EDL7 0-6-2 LNER Tank Locomotive No.9596, in green, generally good plus contained in plain dark blue box. Sold for £80, Vectis, March.

Hornby Dublo OO Gauge 3-Rail GWR 0-6-2T Locomotive, in GWR green as No. 6699, horseshow magnet chassis, 'Hornby' cast on smokebox door, very good in non-original box. Sold for £160, Special Auction Services, April.

Wrenn OO Gauge W2227/A 'Sir William Stanier' in LMS black No. 6256, in original box, stamped Packer No. 3, very good to excellent. Sold for £160, Special Auction Services, April.

Hornby Dublo OO Gauge 3-Rail Stanier 8F Locomotive, late version in BR black as 48094, very good, in original box. Sold for £230, Special Auction Services, April.

Hornby Dublo 2-rail 4076 6-wheeled Passenger Brake "Stove" M32958, in maroon/red, generally excellent, box good plus. Sold for £100, Vectis, April.

Hornby Dublo OO Gauge 3-Rail 3221 BR green 5002 'Ludlow Castle' Locomotive and Tender, in original box, fair to good but grubby, box passable to fair. Sold for £190, Special Auction Services, April.

Trix Twin 3-rail 277 3-Car Diesel Flyer, in red and cream. Good plus to excellent in poor box. Sold for £60, Vectis, March.

Hornby Dublo OO Gauge 3-Rail 2-6-4T Locomotive, late version in BR black as 80059, very good, in original box. Sold for £250, Special Auction Services, April.

Wrenn Railways BR Green 34051 'Winston Churchill' 4-6-2 Locomotive and Tender No. W2265, mint in excellent plus box. Sold for £240, Warwick & Warwick, May.

Wrenn W2266 4-6-2 Loco and Tender West Country Class 'Plymouth' Southern Green No.21C103, near mint in box, base coded 08311. Includes instructions. Sold for £190, Vectis, March.

Wrenn W2308 2-8-0 Loco and Tender BR Green Class 8F No.48102, near mint in good box with reproduction base. Includes instructions. Sold for £500, Vectis, March.

Wrenn W2262 4-6-0 Loco and Tender Royal Scot Class BR Green 'Grenadier Guardsman' No.46110, near mint in good plus box with instructions. Sold for £140, Vectis, March.

Wrenn W2241/A 4-6-2 Loco and Tender Duchess Class LMS Black 'Duchess of Gloucester' No.6225, near mint to mint in good plus box with instructions. Sold for £120, Vectis, March.

Hornby Dublo BR Maroon E1939 Restaurant Car No. 4071 nearly mint in nearly excellent box with small price sticker to front. Sold for £85, Warwick & Warwick, March.

Wrenn W2247A 4-6-0 Loco and Tender BR Green "Clun Castle" No.7029 near mint to mint in excellent box, base coded 91 1 3. Includes instructions. Sold for £580, Vectis, March.

Wrenn W2290 4-6-2 Loco and Tender Southern Green Merchant Navy Class 'Canadian Pacific, No.21C5, near mint to mint in excellent plus to near mint box, base coded 90626. Includes instructions. Sold for £280, Vectis, March.

Hornby Dublo 2-rail 4076 6-wheeled Passenger Brake Van 'Stove' No. M32958, in maroon, in original box. General condition is excellent, box good plus. Sold for £70, Vectis, June.

Hornby O Gauge Clockwork Southern Green 2091 No. 2 Special Tank 4-4-2 Locomotive, slight cracking to some small wheels, no key buy in good working order, generally good in incorrect box LNER box. Sold for £110, Warwick & Warwick, May.

Hornby Dublo BR Green D5702 Class 28 Co-Bo Diesel Locomotive No. 2233, nearly mint with orange test label, original body card protectors, in excellent plus box. Sold for £75, Warwick & Warwick, March.

Bassett-Lowke O gauge Standard Tank 0-6-0 electric 12v DC tank locomotive LNER 8937, black No. 5305/0 with red lining, about excellent in good plus box (signs of water damage). Sold for £240, Warwick & Warwick, July.

Bassett-Lowke LNER 1931 series brake end coach No. 62362, minor marks to roof and some re-touching, sides excellent. Good condition, box fair. Sold for £100, Lacy, Scott & Knight, August.

Bassett-Lowke O gauge electric LMS maroon 1063 Standard Compound 4-4-0 locomotive and tender No. 5302/0, generally excellent plus, missing number from smoke box door, in good plus box. Sold for £230, Warwick & Warwick, July.

Bassett-Lowke post-war 'blood & custard' first class BR coach, good, box good. Sold for £95, Lacy, Scott & Knight, August.

— not applicable —

DIECAST RAILWAYS TOY FIGURES TINPLATE TV & FILM OTHERS EBUYS

Hornby Dublo 3-rail locomotive and tender EDL11 4-6-2 Class A4 'Silver King' No. 60016, in green livery, boxed locomotive, unboxed tender. Sold for £80, Vectis, June.

Bassett-Lowke Winteringham orange NE brake van, small chips to roof, good to very good. Sold for £80, Lacy, Scott & Knight, August.

Bassett-Lowke O gauge electric LMS maroon 2945 Stanier Mogul 2-6-0 locomotive and tender No. 4601/0, largely re-painted, good plus, in hand made wooden box. Sold for £190, Warwick & Warwick, July.

Bassett-Lowke Winteringham LMS brake van, some re-touching to sides, good, box passable. Sold for £80, Lacy, Scott & Knight, August.

Wrenn Railways LMS black 6102 Black Watch 4-6-0 No. W2261, mint in excellent box. Sold for £160, Warwick & Warwick, July.

Wrenn Railways W2213 4-6-2 locomotive and tender NE black A4 class 'Peregrine' No. 4903, excellent to excellent plus in good box. Sold for £70, Vectis, June.

Wrenn Railways W2236 4-6-2 locomotive and tender rebuilt West Country class 'Dorchester' BR green No. 34024, good plus to excellent in fair to good box. Sold for £70, Vectis, June.

Bassett-Lowke Winteringham LMS cattle van, minor rust mark to one side, roof re-painted. Good, box good. Sold for £80, Lacy, Scott & Knight, August.

Wrenn Railways BR class 20 Bo-Bo, mint in excellent plus box. Sold for £32, Warwick & Warwick, July.

Bassett-Lowke wooden goods depot with sliding doors, including 11 tinplate advertising signs but missing the goods depot sign. Good condition. Sold for £75, Lacy, Scott & Knight, August.

Hornby Dublo BR green 34005 Barnstaple Rebuilt 'West Country' Class 4-6-2 E776 locomotive and tender No. 2235, good plus in good box. Sold for £60, Warwick & Warwick, July.

Hornby Dublo 3-rail EDL7 Tank Locomotive 0-6-2 No. 2594, in Southern green, generally excellent, box good plus (missing inserts). Sold for £340, Vectis, June.

Bassett-Lowke O gauge electric LMS maroon 1082 Standard Compound 4-4-0 locomotive and tender No. 5302/0, generally good plus, re-touched in places, in good plus box. Sold for £160, Warwick & Warwick, July.

Trix Twin 3-rail EM1 Bo-Bo Overhead Eletric Locomotive BR black No. 26010, good plus in reproduction box. Sold for £70, Vectis, June.

Wrenn Railways W2287 4-6-2 locomotive and tender rebuilt West Country class 'Westward Ho' BR green No. 34036, near mint to mint in excellent box. Sold for £260, Vectis, June.

Wrenn Railways BR green 46235 City of Birmingham Duchess Class 4-6-2 locomotive and tender No. W2228, mint in nearly excellent box, box stamped underneath 'Packer No. 3'. Sold for £65, Warwick & Warwick, July.

Wrenn Railways W2301 4-6-2 locomotive and tender Steamlined Coronation class 'Queen Elizabeth' LMS blue No. 6221, slight paint loss to the underside of the chassis, otherwise near mint in excellent box. Sold for £500, Vectis, June.

Wrenn Railways W2237 4-6-2 locomotive and tender rebuilt West Country class 'Lyme-Regis' No. 21C109, locomotive is excellent, marks to one tender side, otherwise excellent. Box good. Sold for £90, Vectis, June.

Bassett-Lowke by Corgi O gauge electric BR black 31407 N Class Mogul 2-6-0 locomotive and tender No. BL99004, nearly mint in about mint box. Sold for £280, Warwick & Warwick, July.

Bassett-Lowke 12v DC BR green 4-6-2 'Flying Scotsman' No. 60103, corrosion marks to top of boiler and cab roof with 'BR' eight wheel tender, crease on front and marks to side. Fair to good. Sold for £400, Lacy, Scott & Knight, August.

Bing maroon LMS clockwork 0-6-0 loco only No. 6508, crazing to body, good condition. Sold for £140, Lacy, Scott & Knight, August.

Wrenn Railways W2241 4-6-2 locomotive and tender Princess Coronation class LMS black 'Duchess of Hamilton' No. 6229, locomotive is near mint, tender has tissue marks to one tender side, otherwise excellent. Box good plus. Sold for £70, Vectis, June.

Hornby No. 4 Wembley Station, made 1940, buff building tin printed speckled platform, some scratches to platform and edge, with ramps, some chips to fencing. Good, box fair. Sold for £80, Lacy, Scott & Knight, August.

Hornby for export dark green LNER clockwork 0-4-0 No. 0 locomotive, 1938-41, '4797' on cabside revised body style, some small chips, with four wheel dark green SAR/SAS tender, small chips and touching in to inside. Good condition. Sold for £220, Lacy, Scott & Knight, August.

Wrenn Railways W2236/A 4-6-2 locomotive and tender rebuilt West Country class 'Bodmin' BR green No. 34016, version with black nameplate, near mint in good plus box. Sold for £240, Vectis, June.

Hornby No. 1 LNWR passenger coach, 1921-23, brass lettered doors, nickel wheels with thick axles/couplings, scratches and dents to roof, one buffer replaced. Fair condition. Sold for £60, Lacy, Scott & Knight, August.

Wrenn Railways W2209/A 4-6-2 locomotive and tender LNER green A4 class 'Great Snipe' No. 4495, driving cog spinning on axle, marks to side of tender, otherwise excellent in good box. Sold for £130, Vectis, June.

Hornby Dublo 3-rail 3235 West Country Class 4-6-2 Engine and Tender 'Dorchester', a very few minor blemishes, complete with instructions. Near mint, box very good. Sold for £160, Lacy, Scott & Knight, May.

Hornby lattice girder bridge, 1928-33, extensive loss of paint but suitable for restoration, passable to fair. Sold for £90, Lacy, Scott & Knight, August.

Hornby Dublo 3250 3-rail Surburban Electric Motor Coach Only, with instrutions and testing certificate. Mint, box mint. Sold for £230, Lacy, Scott & Knight, May.

Hornby Pratts Petrol tank wagon, 1934-36, lighter orange, standard base with pressed filler, a few small chips, good to very good. Sold for £60, Lacy, Scott & Knight, August.

Wrenn Railways W2311 4-6-2 locomotive and tender BR black Princess Coronation class 'City of Leeds' No. 46244, near mint, box creased to one end, otherwise good plus to excellent. Sold for £560, Vectis, June.

Wrenn Railways W2266 4-6-2 locomotive and tender Steamlined West Country class 'Plymouth' Southern green No. 21C103, tissue marks to one tender side, otherwise near mint in a good plus to excellent box. Sold for £150, Vectis, June.

Wrenn Railways W2265 BR Green 'Winston Churchill' Engine Tender, with instructions, 'packer No. 1' on box base. Mint, box near mint. Sold for £250, Lacy, Scott & Knight, May.

Wrenn Railways W2227/A LMP Postwar Black 'Sir William Stanier FRS' Engine and Tender, with instructions. Mint. Sold for £140, Lacy, Scott & Knight, May.

Wrenn Railways W2242 LMS maroon 'City of Liverpool', engine and tender, mint, box good. Sold for £95, Lacy, Scott & Knight, August.

Wrenn Railways W2289 4-6-2 locomotive and tender Steamlined Merchant Navy Class in Southern Black 'Canadian Pacific' No. 21C5, near mint to mint in near mint box. Sold for £400, Vectis, June.

Hornby Dublo OO Gauge 3-Rail 3234 Diesel Electric Locomotive D9001 'St Paddy', in BR two-tone green, with original box. Good condition, a little grubby and lacks paperwork. Sold for £210, Special Auction Services, April.

Hornby Dublo 2-rail 2220 Locomotive and Tender of a 4-6-0 Castle Class Locomotive Denbigh Castle No.7032, in green livery in plain box with label, good plus. Sold for £110, Vectis, March.

Wrenn Railways LMS Black 6256 Sir William A. Stainer FRS 4-6-2 Locomotive and Tender No. W2227A, mint in excellent box with instructions. Sold for £120, Warwick & Warwick, March.

Wrenn Railways W2225 2-8-0 locomotive and tender LMS black class '8F' No. 8042, excellent in good box. Sold for £50, Vectis, June.

Bassett-Lowke by Corgi LMS maroon 6201 Princess Elizabeth 4-6-2 locomotive and tender No. BL99006, mint, unused in excellent plus box with outer carton. Sold for £440, Warwick & Warwick, July.

Wrenn Railways W2239 4-6-2 locomotive and tender BR green rebuilt West Country class 'Eddystone' No. 34028, version with closed up nameplate, slight tissue marking to one tender side, otherwise near mint in excellent box. Sold for £100, Vectis, June.

Bassett-Lowke by Corgi O gauge electric LMS black 6210 Lady Patricia 4-6-2 locomotive and tender No. BL99010, nearly mint, extra weights have been fixed under the body, in excellent plus box. Sold for £350, Warwick & Warwick, July.

DIECAST   RAILWAYS   TOY FIGURES   TINPLATE   TV & FILM   OTHERS   EBUYS

Toy Figures

Introduction to...

Toy figures cover a huge range of categories - from World War II to Arctic adventures!

Rather like model railways, toy soldiers/ figures are a collectable that has been around for decades and there's even a famous photograph of Abraham Lincoln playing with some toy soldiers alongside his son Tad. In some ways it's easy to see why toy soldiers have been such a long-standing aspect of growing up, particularly for boys... and that's because young lads just love playing 'war'. Whether it's with a stick in the garden or a toy soldier in the living room, the opportunity to recreate spectacular battles in relative safety is just too much to resist for young minds.

Of course, once upon a time the material of choice for all these toy soldiers was lead – to hell with the potential poisoning! But since then manufacturers have moved to plastic or white metal, to ensure that little Timmy doesn't snuff it after swallowing a miniature bayonet. As a result, you'll find that most of the early examples are made of lead, while from the 1950s onwards more manufacturers began to experiment with the 'futuristic' material known as plastic.

In terms of collecting, toy soldiers aren't quite as popular as they once were and, whereas once upon time, they were probably up there with diecast and model railways in terms of auction lots, now they are sadly lower down the pecking order. However, that's not to say they're no longer valuable and dedicated collectors will happily pay hundreds, if not thousands for those rare early pieces. In fact, even some of the plastic examples are steadily increasing in price as they mature in age – a bit like a fine wine.

Obviously the name that dominates this category is Britains and most of the items sold through auction will have come from the British manufacturer. Rather like Hornby has become synonymous with railways, it's hard to think of toy soldiers without the name 'Britains' escaping from your lips. Incredibly Britains was founded way back in 1893 and revolutionised the toy soldier industry with the introduction of hollowcasting, which meant that lead figures no longer had to be solid metal and instead could have a hollow inner. The result was that producing the models was cheaper and, more importantly, the models were lighter once in the grubby hands of eager children.

The problem is that these enthusiastic playtimes meant that paint would regularly get chipped off early lead examples, so finding these in mint condition is no easy task – as reflected in the price. Likewise boxed examples command a premium because these were typically thrown away as the figure was added to the battalion ready for war!

One of the solutions to this problem came with the introduction of plastic in the 1950s. Although the models were much lighter they could withstand the rigors of playtimes a little better, meaning more have survived in good condition. On the flipside there are rare colour variations in these plastic pieces – particularly the Swoppets from Britains – and these are very sought after. Perhaps one of the most attractive aspects of figure collecting is the huge amount of themes - from spacemen to cowboys, you're likely to find something to tickle your fancy. ∎

124

This year we've rounded up 124 metal and plastic figures.

54

Our average price paid for a toy figure has dropped 54% this year - although we have listed more items.

£94

Never an exact science but the average price paid was £94.

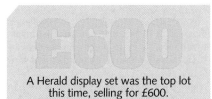

£600

A Herald display set was the top lot this time, selling for £600.

£11,595

This year's total amount for toy figures is £11,595 - down on last year's £19k.

Little Wars

After H. G. Wells' book on the rules of wargaming recently celebrated its cetenary, we review this famous work, which kickstarted the wargames industry.

H. G. Wells is probably best known for his wonderful works of science fiction. Whether it's Martians invading Earth in War of the Worlds, a scientist turning himself invisible in *The Invisible Man* or strange animal creations in the *Island of Dr. Moreau*, H. G. Wells has an incredible talent for creating fantastic works of fiction. However, did you also know he wrote books establishing rules for miniature wargaming? Well he did and, in fact, he wrote two: *Floor Games* and, the more substantial, *Little Wars*.

Written in 1913, *Little Wars* is "a game for boys from twelve years of age to one hundred and fifty and for that more intelligent sort of girl who likes boys' games and books". It spells out some pretty simple rules for fighting between infantry, cavalry and artillery, along with using a 4.7-inch toy naval gun to launch projectiles to destroy enemy soldiers or buildings. As well as describing the rules, Wells, who was also a well known pacifist, gives his thoughts on warfare in general and, as such, is still an interesting read even for those not interested in playing the game itself.

Wells begins by describing how he came up with the basis for *Little Wars* and the origins certainly have all the hallmarks of a Victorian gent. While having lunch with a friend and waiting for coffee in a room "littered with the irrepressible debris of a small boy's pleasures" – in other words a bunch of toy soldiers – Wells' pal picked up a toy naval gun and shot a small projectile at the soldiers, knocking one over. From these humble beginnings, Wells goes on to say that "he fired a shot that day that still echoes round the

There are more modern rules for Little Wars that include additions such as railways and tanks, as shown in the background here.

world" and so *Little Wars* began to take shape.

Originally Wells says: "We got two forces of toy soldiers set out a lumpish Encyclopaedic land upon the carpet, and began to play. We arranged to move in alternate moves: first one moved all his force and then the other; an infantry-man could move one foot at each move, a cavalry-man two, a gun two, and it might fire six shots; and if a man was moved up to touch another man, then we tossed up and decided which man was dead. So we made a game, which was not a good game, but which was very amusing once or

twice."

Other improvements quickly followed, including the development of a 'country' for the battles to take place in. Instead of a few books, Wells decided it was best to use wooden playing bricks to represent buildings and cover, twigs became mighty forests and ponds or lakes were chalked out on the floor. It was also decided that one player should be tasked with laying out the country before the game, while the other chooses his side.

The next decision came regarding the movement of "that wild and fearful fowl, the gun".

Wells decided that a gun could not be fired unless there were four men within six inches of it (to represent the crew) and that it could not both fire and move in the same general move. Meanwhile, the gun could move a foot if near an infantry man or two feet if he was a cavalry man. Along with some rules regarding the length of battles and the capturing of prisoners, Wells finally felt his basic rules for wargaming were complete.

"And so our laws all made, battles have been fought, the mere beginnings, we feel, of vast campaigns. The game has

ABOVE The cavalry prepares to charge into action! H. G. Wells carefully maps out the distances units can move in his explaination of the rules.

ABOVE The gun is one of the most important aspects of Little Wars and players must keep them safe. *Images courtesy Funny Little Wars.*

ABOVE When playing outside the scale of warfare can be much bigger, as demonstrated here by Funny Little Wars.

INSET Wells even gave examples of potential set-ups for your miniature battles.

LEFT Of course H. G. Wells recommends British toy soldiers for the game but you can use anything you like on the battlefield.

become in a dozen aspects extraordinarily like a small real battle. In two or three moves the guns are flickering into action, a cavalry melee may be in progress, the plans of the attack are more or less apparent, here are men pouring out from the shelter of a wood to secure some point of vantage, and here are troops massing among farm buildings for a vigorous attack."

Wells, being the fine English gent he was, obviously recommends British toy soldiers, as mentioned when describing the size of the figures that should be used. "The soldiers used should be all of one size. The best British makers have standardised sizes, and sell infantry and cavalry in exactly proportioned dimensions; the infantry being nearly two inches tall. There is a lighter, cheaper make of perhaps an inch and a half high that is also available. Foreign-made soldiers are of variable sizes."

After giving the background to the game, Wells then gives a wonderful account of the 'Battle of Hook's Farm' which starts with this fantastic introduction: "Suddenly your author changes. He changes into what perhaps he might have been—under different circumstances. His inky fingers become large, manly hands, his drooping scholastic back stiffens, his elbows go out, his etiolated complexion corrugates and darkens, his moustaches increase and grow and spread, and curl up horribly; a large, red scar, a sabre cut, grows lurid over one eye. He expands—all over he expands. He clears his throat startlingly, lugs at the still growing ends of his moustache, and says, with just a faint and fading doubt in his voice as to whether he can do it, "Yas, Sir!"" Wells then goes on to call himself H. G. W. of the Blue Army.

Despite *Little Wars* being 100-years-old, it's still played by wargame and toy soldier enthusiasts today and is likely to have formed the basis for many popular tabletop wargames. In fact, many still continue to play games based on the traditional rules and there's a website called Funny Little Wars (garden wargames for the "better sort of chap") which expands the rules with logistics, railways, supply and other facets Wells was considering at the end of *Little Wars*. ■

Britains No.24 9th Queen's Royal Lancers, comprising one officer turned in saddle; four mounted troopers. Appears fair, one with broken neck (head still attached), in fair box with split to side and corner of lid. Sold for £70, Aston's, September.

Britains Types of the Royal Navy set, comprising seven Naval officer figures. Overall good in passable box. Sold for £70, Aston's, September.

Britains Swoppets 15th Century Knights No. 1452 Mounted Knight Attacking with Sword, second version (1963), with green plume on a black horse with white reins and mauve blanket. Mint in a mint blue/yellow pavilion box. Sold for £110, Cottees, September.

Britains Types Of The Argentine Army No.216 Infanteria Argentina, comprising eight infantrymen marching at the slope. Appears fair in passable repaired box. Sold for £70, Aston's, September.

Britains No.1289 The Gun of the Royal Artillery with Officer and Team of Gunners, RA gun finished in khaki, officer with binoculars, three kneeling gunners and three standing gunners. Good to fair, one figure missing feet/base, in fair box. Sold for £120, Aston's, September.

Britains Regiments of All Nations No.2084 Colour Party Of The Scots Guards, comprising six lead figures, including two flag-bearers. Appears good to fair in fair box with a couple of repairs, includes complaint slip. Sold for £50, Aston's, September.

Charbens Strong Man and Barbell, good condition. Sold for £20, Aston's, September.

Britains Parrot on a Perch, good condition. Sold for £45, Aston's, September.

Britains Soldiers Regiments Of All Nations 2111 Black Watch Colour Party, good, dusty and some paint wear, tied into fair box with complaint slip. Sold for £80, Aston's, September.

Two lead Parrots on Perch Stand, one blue, the other red. Good condition. Sold for £80, Aston's, September.

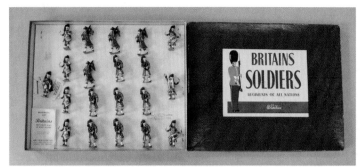

Britains Soldiers Regiments Of All Nations 2109 Pipe Band of the Black Watch, contains 20 figures. Very good, tied into good box with complaint slip and numerical list of Britains catalogue. Sold for £110, Aston's, September.

Morestone Clown and Dog on Penny Farthing, rare, good condition. Sold for £360, Aston's, September.

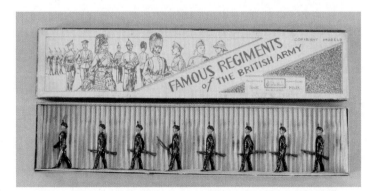

Britains Famous Regiments of the British Army No.2072 Kings Royal Rifle Corps at the Trail, comprising eight figures. Appears good to very good in good box, with hand-written end label. Sold for £55, Aston's, September.

Britains Regiments of All Nations No.66 Indian Army 13th Duke of Connaught's Own Lancers, comprising one mounted trumpeter, four mounted Sowars with lances. Appears very good with some minor paint loss, in good to very good box. Sold for £80, Aston's, September.

DIECAST   RAILWAYS   TOY FIGURES   TINPLATE   TV & FILM   OTHERS   EBUYS

Britains Swoppets No. 532 Indian Brave With Bow Mounted, second issue, in orange/black issue box, in mint boxed condition. Sold for £40, C&T Auctions, October.

Britains Mammoth Circus No.1539 Set, four elephants, four prancing Liberty horses, two trotting Pinto horses, four clowns including two boxing clowns, two tigers, boxing kangaroo, tub, clown on stilts, ringmaster, ballerina with stand, lion tamer and green ring. Overall good to very good in repaired box. Sold for £340, Aston's, September.

Britains Types of the Royal Navy No.35 Royal Marines (Marching), comprising: one marching officer, seven marines marching at the slope. Good plus, officer's arm unattached but present, in good to fair box with tear to side and corner of lid. Sold for £50, Aston's, September.

Britains Regiments of all Nations No.2089 Gloucestershire Regiment, comprising one officer with drawn sword and seven infantry marching at the slope, No.1 dress. Appears good to very good with complaint slip, in good box. Sold for £60, Aston's, September.

Britains Regiments of all Nations No.2178 Fort Henry Guards Band, comprising bandmaster and nine bandsmen with various instrumentation. Appears fair in reproduction box. Sold for £80, Aston's, September.

Britains Swoppets No. 534 Indian With Bow And Arrow Mounted, second issue, brown horse, in orange/black issue box, in mint boxed condition. Sold for £40, C&T Auctions, October.

Britains Zoo No. 905 Large Hippopotamus, good in fair box. Sold for £30, Aston's, September.

Britains Swoppets H535 Indian Brave With Tomahawk Mounted, first issue, with green/black issue box, Herald Swoppets card tag in mint condition, box has age wear. Sold for £40, C&T Auctions, October.

Britains Knights of Agincourt No.1661, mounted knight on charging destrier horse (red caparison) with shield and lance. Very good plus with complaint slip in very good stone-effect box. Sold for £85, Aston's, September.

Britains No.1257 The Yeomen Of The Guard, comprising eight Beefeaters with pikes and officer with cane. Appears good in fair box with some repairs. Sold for £60, Aston's, September.

Britains No.1448 Army Staff Car, khaki green with driver and passenger some restoration in fair box. Sold for £120, Aston's, September.

Britains Swoppets No. 635 Cowboy Wounded With Arrow Mounted, in orange/black issue box, in excellent boxed condition. Sold for £35, C&T Auctions, October.

Britains No.39 Royal Horse Artillery with Gun and Escort, comprising six horse team at the gallop, three have drivers with extended whip arms, four mounted gunners holding Carbines, mounted officer, gun and limber, plus traces. Good plus in fair box with repaired lid. 'Directions' to inside of lid. Sold for £130, Aston's, September.

Britains Swoppets No. 635 Cowboy Wounded With Arrow Mounted, in red/black issue box, in near mint boxed condition, box has slight age wear, no label to end flap. Sold for £30, C&T Auctions, October.

Britains Swoppets No. 640 Cowboy Prisoner Mounted, in orange/black issue box, in mint boxed condition. Sold for £60, C&T Auctions, October.

Britains Swoppets No. 634 Cowboy Firing Rifle Mounted, in orange/black issue box, in excellent boxed condition. Sold for £35, C&T Auctions, October.

Britains Set 2 Womens Royal Army Corps, very good in fair box with repro labels to lid. Sold for £80, Aston's, September.

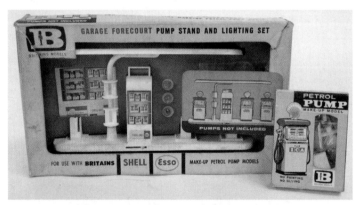

Britains No. 4260 Garage Forecourt Pump Stand & lighting Set, in mint condition, box has age wear, missing acetate window, plus 1261 Shell petrol pump mint boxed. Sold for £75, C&T Auctions, October.

Britains Knights of Agincourt No.1659, mounted knight on charging destrier horse (blue and red caparison) with shield and mace. Very good with complaint slip in very good stone-effect box. Sold for £85, Aston's, September.

Britains Knights of Agincourt No.1660, mounted knight on charging destrier horse (blue and yellow caparison) with shield and sword. Very good plus with complaint slip in very good stone-effect box. Sold for £85, Aston's, September.

Britains Scarce Garage Forecourts Set, three plastic petrol pumps and stand, in mint condition, box has age wear. Sold for £60, C&T Auctions, October.

Britains Knights of Agincourt No.1662, mounted knight on destrier horse (blue caparison) with St. George flag. Very good plus in good to very good stone-effect box with small surface tear to lid. Sold for £85, Aston's, September.

Scarce John Hillco Miniature Lorry and Gas Cylinders, olive green body, with silver gas cylinders (for Barrage Balloon) in near mint condition, with original tissue paper, complete with original card box with printed label. Sold for £80, C&T Auctions, October.

DIECAST RAILWAYS TOY FIGURES TINPLATE TV & FILM OTHERS EBUYS

Britains Historical Series No.1258 Tournament Knights, comprising two mounted knights carrying lances, one mounted marshall, one herald on foot and two squires on foot holding staffs. Appears good, with complaint slip, in good box with Historical Series label. Sold for £90, Aston's, September.

Britains Swoppets 15th Century Knights No. 1452 Mounted Knight Attacking with Sword, second version (1963), with green plume on a brown horse with yellow reins and red strap. Mint in a second issue blue/yellow pavilion box. Sold for £120, Cottees, September.

Britains Swoppets 15th Century Knights No. 1451 Mounted Knight Charging with Red Lance, second version (1963), with yellow plume on a brown horse with light blue reins and blue blanket. Mint in a mint second issue red/yellow pavilion box. Sold for £110, Cottees, September.

Britains Swoppets 15th Century Knights No. 1452 Mounted Knight with Sword, first version (1959), with light blue plume on a brown horse with white reins and blue blanket. Mint in an excellent first issue red-striped tent-style box with Britains Herald logo to base. Sold for £170, Cottees, September.

Britains Swoppets 15th Century Knights No. 1450 Mounted Knight with Red Rose Standard, first version (1959), with yellow plume on a white horse with white reins and red strap. Mint in a mint first issue red-striped tent-style box Sold for £190, Cottees, September.

FG Taylor & Sons No. 811 Chariot Set, pale green chariot with red spoked wheels, Roman driver in red with whip and gold cape, two white horses with reins. Good in a good to fair Mid-West British Importers box. Sold for £70, Aston's, September.

Britains Wartime Issue Set 'Types of the British Army' box with 'Churchill' end label, contains six Militiamen, set 185, six figures at the slope and one empty handed officer with black side cap. Only listed 1940-4. Very good in good box with correct card insert. Sold for £300, Aston's, September.

Britains Swoppets 15th Century Knights No. 1452 Mounted Knight Attacking with Sword, second version (1963), with yellow plume on a black horse with white reins and red strap. Mint in a mint second issue red/yellow pavilion box. Sold for £130, Cottees, September.

Britains No.2017 Ski Troops, four skiers with poles and skis. Very good in very good box (repaired corner of label to lid). Together with three Johillco Arctic Explorer style figures, appear very good but unboxed. Sold for £180, Aston's, September.

Benbros 'AA' Motor Cycle and Side Car, black motorcycle, yellow hinged lid side car with black aerial, windscreen shield, driver dressed in green and black. Length 8.5cm. Good to fair condition with some paint chips, in good to fair box with repaired inner end flap and tear to one side. Sold for £60, Aston's, September.

Britains Swoppets 15th Century Knights No. 1453 Mounted Knight Defending with Blue Lance, first version (1959), with green plume on a white horse with light blue reins and mauve blanket. Mint in an excellent first issue blue-striped tent-style box. Sold for £190, Cottees, September.

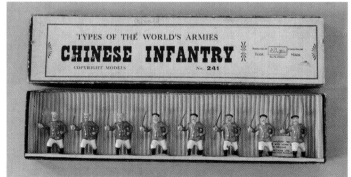

Britains No.241 Chinese Infantry, eight infantry with raised swords, in green, blue, or red jacket with white trousers. Appear good to fair in good to fair box with a couple of punctures to lid. Sold for £140, Aston's, September.

Kemlow (England) Fairground Dodgem Car, red with number '90' to rear, wheels, two seated girls. Length 8cm, height 8cm. Good to fair. Sold for £220, Aston's, September.

Pixyland Kew lead Cricket Umpire, as seen in the 1928 Cricketers Set, wearing white coat with farm trousers and dark brown cap, rare example with some losses. Sold for £35, Lacy, Scott & Knight, November.

Britains Deetail No. 7348 British and German Infantry, 22 assorted soldiers in various stances, in original window box, box is heavily faded and window is split. Sold for £55, Lacy, Scott & Knight, November.

Britains Swoppets 15th Century Knights No. 1453 Mounted Knight Defending with Blue Lance, second version (1963), with green plume on a black horse with white reins and purple blanket. Mint in a mint second issue blue/yellow pavilion box. Sold for £130, Cottees, September.

Britains No.782 Suffolk Punch mare, brown body with grey hoofs and ribbon decoration to tail, rare example, some losses. Sold for £35, Lacy, Scott & Knight, November.

Britains Eyes Right Regimental Models Set 7499 Band of the US Marines, band master and 19 marching musicians playing various instruments. Near mint overall, contained in a generally very good window display box. Rare Issue. Sold for £100, Vectis, November.

Britains No.109 The Royal Dublin Fusiliers, comprising eight soldiers. Overall good in good bright green Whisstock label campaign box. Sold for £80, Aston's, September.

Britains 7316 Britains Zoo Animals set, comprising 10 assorted zoo animals, a quantity of green fencing and internal zoo card, in the original window box with blue sliding interior tray. Very good to near mint. Sold for £50, Lacy, Scott & Knight, November.

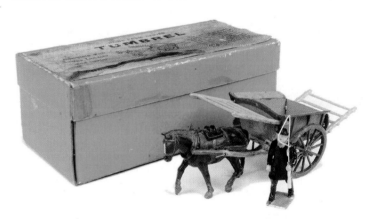

Britains Set 4F Tumbrel Cart (Pre War version), brown horse, mustard yellow cart with red spoked wheels, cream hay racks and carter with whip in black smock. Some paint loss and damages otherwise generally fair overall. Sold for £40, Vectis, November.

Britains Swoppets 15th Century Knights No. 1453 Mounted Knight Defending with Blue Lance, second version (1963), with green plume on a black horse with yellow reins and blue blanket. Mint in a mint second issue blue/yellow pavilion box. Sold for £120, Cottees, September.

Unconfirmed US maker Space Men, comprising astronaut, robot and three space vehicles. Generally near mint overall, strung on a generally excellent illustrated space rocket shaped header card. Sold for £170, Vectis, November.

Timpo Solids Set Ref: 210/1 Cowboys & Indians Range, circa, 1958, comprising: four Indians on foot - one damaged. Some paint loss otherwise generally excellent overall, now contained in a generally excellent contemporary Timpo 1950s style pictorial set box. Sold for £30, Vectis, November.

DIECAST   RAILWAYS   TOY FIGURES   TINPLATE   TV & FILM   OTHERS   EBUYS

Clarke's Toys and Novelties Limited Series 201 Station Equipment set, comprising bench, truck, suitcase, sack barrow and figure, in the original red and buff coloured box, box heavily worn. Sold for £40, Lacy, Scott & Knight, November.

Timpo Series Eight Silver Knights, first version, second issues (1965/66), comprising five mounted knights with weapons, mounted on second issue 'Swoppet' type horses with separate bridles and caparisons. Near mint overall, contained in a plain red box. Sold for £60, Vectis, November.

Britains (Herald) Swoppets Cowboys & Indians Series Set H 533 Indian Chief with Dagger - Mounted, generally very good overall, contained in an excellent (minor age wear overall) first issue green/black illustrated box. Sold for £20, Vectis, November.

Britains Swoppets 15th Century Knights No. 1452 Mounted Knight Attacking with Sword, mounted on a brown horse. This example is complete with a red caparison. Generally near mint, contained in a generally near mint second issue pavilion type window box. Sold for £80, Vectis, November.

Britains Swoppets 15th Century Knights No. 1450 Mounted Knight with Standard, mounted on a brown horse. This example is complete with a yellow caparison. Generally near mint, contained in a near mint second issue box. Sold for £60, Vectis, November.

Britains Swoppets 15th Century Knights H.1451 Mounted Knight Charging with Lance, mounted on a rearing brown horse. This example is complete with a yellow caparison. Near mint, contained in a near mint pavilion type window box. Sold for £110, Vectis, November.

Britains Swoppets 15th Century Knights H.1452 Mounted Knight Attacking with Sword, near excellent overall, contained in a generally good (age wear - fragile) first issue 'solid' type pavilion red/blue type box. Rare, first issue. Sold for £110, Vectis, November.

Britains Swoppets 15th Century Knights H.1450 Mounted Knight with Standard, near excellent overall, contained in a generally good (age wear - fragile). First issue 'solid' type pavilion red/blue type box. Rare, first issue Sold for £70, Vectis, November.

Cherilea 60mm 'Swoppet' Range Wild West Series, comprising cowboys: one mounted, four on foot with various weapons and cactus scenic piece. Near mint overall, contained in a generally excellent window set box. Sold for £35, Vectis, November.

Britains Eyes Right Set 7273 Royal Marines, comprising officer marching with drawn sword, 10 marines marching at the slope and sentry box. Near mint overall, contained in a generally excellent (minor age wear) yellow and black window display box. Sold for £130, Vectis, November.

Britains Ancient Siege Machines Series Set 4675 Catapult, medieval catapult, two crew and projectiles (three missing). Generally excellent overall, contained in a very good illustrated card box with internal plinth display. Sold for £30, Vectis, November.

Britains Herald H. 5499 Robin Hood and his Merrie Men display card (1957), comprising: Robin Hood, Little John, Friar Tuck and Maid Marian. Some minor paint chips otherwise near mint overall, contained on an excellent (minor age wear) pictorial open card display with raised titles to the front. An exceptionally rare set in this packaging format. Sold for £480, Vectis, November.

Herald Model No. H520 Mounted Indian Chief (1956 issue), near mint overall, contained in a generally excellent (some minor age wear) first issue illustrated box marked "Zang Product" to base. Sold for £130, Vectis, November.

Britains Deetail metal based models, six-piece Indian calvary group, including six various Indians in various stances, all housed on original back card display stand. Good to very good. Sold for £60, Lacy, Scott & Knight, November.

Britains (Herald) Swoppets Cowboys & Indians Series H631 Cowboy Bank Robber - Mounted, some minor paint loss otherwise generally very good and complete, contained in a generally excellent (minor age wear) first issue red/black illustrated box. Sold for £20, Vectis, November.

Timpo Swoppets Series 25 Knights of the Middle Ages (Helm Knights) Mounted Helm Knight, with red/blue diamond insignia complete with original 'green star' banner. Mint. Extremely rare to find complete with banner. Sold for £25, Vectis, November.

Herald English Civil War Series Set H.4408 Roundhead Trooper and Cavalier Musketeer, near mint overall, contained on a near mint grey and maroon Herald Models "Half Moon" type display card. Rare to find in this condition. Sold for £600, Vectis, November.

Britains Herald Set H.5298 Polar Survey Party (1958 - 62), some minor paint loss otherwise generally very good overall. Un-boxed. Sold for £40, Vectis, November.

Herald Model No. H620 Mounted Cowboy Lassoing (1956 issue), some minor paint loss otherwise generally excellent overall, contained in a generally excellent (minor age wear) first issue illustrated box marked "Zang Product" to base. Sold for £110, Vectis, November.

Crescent Toys lead Dunce Girl, in yellow dress with yellow dunce hat, brown plaited hair with red bow, some fatigue. Sold for £60, Lacy, Scott & Knight, November.

Britains Pre-War lead 887B Rare Man in Panama hat, from Railway Set No. 168, near mint. Sold for £55, Lacy, Scott & Knight, November.

Timpo Model Zoo Set 401, 1950s issue, including oryx, zebra, moose, two birds, squirrel on tree, keeper and keeper with brush. Near mint overall in generally very good box. Sold for £80, Vectis, March.

Crescent No. 1600 The Circus, 1960s issue, including ring master, two clowns, strongman, two equestriennes, two performing lions and two horses. Mint contained in a generally excellent window box. Sold for £60, Vectis, March.

Timpo American Civil War Range Set 30777/6/2 Confederate Soldiers, 1970 issue, comprising four horse gun team, two seated gunners, cannon, Confederate cavalrymen and Confederate infantrymen. Mint overall. Sold for £340, Vectis, March.

Timpo Modern Army Series Ref. 309 Bazooka Set, 1972 issue, including German infantrymen, US bazooka crew and spare ammunition, tree and ruined wall section. Mint overall in excellent box. Sold for £60, Vectis, March.

Britains 7434 Confederate Gun Team & Limber Set, 1st issue in window display box, model is in near mint condition, box has age wear, window acetate is loose in box. Sold for £70, C&T Auctioneers, April.

Two Timpo Modern Army Series Sets, 268 Infantry and 308 Underwater Submarine, both in window boxes, figures are mint, boxes have age wear Sold for £60, C&T Auctioneers, April.

Timpo Tip Tops Frozen North Series, 44049 Eskimo Igloo with three Eskimo Hunters and Polar Bear, figures are mint, box has some age wear. Sold for £30, C&T Auctioneers, April.

Scarce Boxed Britains Set H- 7520 Swoppet Indians, Brave with bow, Brave with tomahawk, both mounted and Chief with spear, Medicine man, both on foot, figures are in mint condition, green/black/white window box (box has been re-cellophaned). Sold for £160, C&T Auctioneers, April.

Scarce Timpo Wild West Series Lead Ranch Set 250, circa 1950s - 14 piece Cowboy and Indian lead figure set, still tied in box, figures are in mint condition, with original box (box has some age wear). Sold for £200, C&T Auctioneers, April.

Timpo Set 2016/8/2 Medieval Knights, circa 1968, including two mounted knights and eight foot knights in assorted poses and liveries. Mint, contained in a generally excellent Timpo Model Toys window box. Sold for £300, Vectis, March.

Britains 4675 Ancient Siege Machines 'Catapult', complete with two medieval soldiers, stone shot still on sprue, in card display box, in near mint condition, box is excellent. Sold for £40, C&T Auctioneers, April.

Britains Model Farm Set 120F, contains two lambs, two hens, five sheep, four cows and horse, figures mint condition, still tied in box, in a very good green lidded box, with label, some slight sun fading to box, still a very nice example. Sold for £220, C&T Auctioneers, April.

Britains (Herald) Racing Cyclists Trade Box for No. 1292 Racing Cyclist Standing, depicted in first style gloss paint, near mint overall, contained in generally excellent Herald trade box. Sold for £60, Vectis, March.

Britains 7616 Wild West Pioneer Covered Wagon, blue wagon, with red wheels, white tilts with flaming arrows, driver and man firing rifle, in excellent unboxed condition. Sold for £30, C&T Auctioneers, April.

Timpo Wild West Collection, 759 Gatling Gun plus two standing Confederates soldiers, mint boxed. Sold for £40, C&T Auctioneers, April.

Timpo Farm Collection, 727 Farmer, Farmer's Wife and assorted farm animals, figures are in mint condition, box has slight age wear. Sold for £45, C&T Auctioneers, April.

Crescent Set 1231 Fish Shop, comprising blue fish fryer with polished tin surround/covers, wooden counter missing, fish shop owner, two customers, scoops, chips and sign. Generally excellent overall in very good box. Sold for £90, Vectis, March.

Britains Eyes Right Models 7243 Band Of The Scots Guards, Drum Major and 12 marching bandsmen playing various instruments, mint boxed, in blue/yellow/white window display box (box has slight age wear). Sold for £45, C&T Auctioneers, April.

Crescent Farm Series Set 1527, early 1950s issue, including farmer, milk maid, cow, young horse, sheep, pig, dog and hedge. Excellent overall in a generally very good box. Sold for £50, Vectis, March.

Britains Eyes Right Models 4283 The Royal Marines Bandsmen, Fife, Drum Major and French Horn, figures are in mint condition, box has age wear. Sold for £20, C&T Auctioneers, April.

Timpo Wild West Series Mounted Cowboy (fatigue-brown horse) WW2006, in excellent condition, with multi-coloured card box, which has slight age wear, complete with all end flaps. Sold for £30, C&T Auctioneers, April.

Timpo Farm Series, including brown and white cow with calf, black and white cow with three calves, bush and tree. Near mint overall, in a generally fair to good box. Sold for £60, Vectis, March.

Timpo Wild West Series Mounted Cowboy (fatigue-black horse) WW2006, in excellent condition, with multi-coloured card box, which has slight age wear, complete with all end flaps. Sold for £30, C&T Auctioneers, April.

Timpo Wild West Series Mounted Cowboy (two guns) WW2000, in excellent condition, with multi-coloured card box, which has some age wear, complete with all end flaps. Sold for £35, C&T Auctioneers, April.

Timpo Wild West Series Buffalo Bill WW2002, in excellent condition, with multi-coloured card box, which has some age wear, complete with all end flaps. Sold for £30, C&T Auctioneers, April.

Crescent Deep Sea Diver Set, including diver in grey diving suit, brass/copper helmet, compressor with airline, bollards, two diver's knives and diver's hatchet. Generally excellent in a generally fair to good box. Sold for £240, Vectis, March.

PP (Popular Plastics) No. P55 The Western Series, including two wheeled covered wagon with two horse team and two drivers, plus four mounted indians. Mint, contained in a near mint box. Sold for £25, Vectis, March.

Timpo Knights of the Middles Ages Set, including mounted helm knight with lance, crusader on foot, medieval tent in pale blue/yellow with red trim and paper liveried flag, plus bush. Mint, contained in a generally excellent Historic Series box. Sold for £100, Vectis, March.

Crescent Railway Personnel Set, including station master, porter with trolley, porter empty handed, guard with flag, engineer and two platform machines. Generally near mint overall, in a generally fair to good box. Sold for £60, Vectis, March.

Britains Eyes Right American Civil War Cavalry No. 451 Federal Cavalry Standard Bearer, near mint overall, contained in generally excellent first issue Herald Series mounted figure set box. Rare first production batch packaging. Sold for £40, Vectis, March.

Britains (Herald) Racing Cyclists No. 1295 Racing Cyclist Sprinting, this is the rare Tour de France 'yellow jersey' version, bottles missing and minor paint loss. Sold for £30, Vectis, March.

Crescent Farm Series Set 1527, late 1950s issue, including farmer with pitch fork, cow, goat, sheep and dog. Generally near mint overall in a generally very good box. Sold for £40, Vectis, March.

Britains War Of Independence Bi-Centennial Anniversary Limited Edition Set no 5156 (1776-1976), six British Infantry, in mint boxed condition. Sold for £40, C&T Auctioneers, April.

Britains Swoppets 15th Century Knights No. 1452 Mounted Knight Attacking with Sword, mounted on a brown horse, complete with yellow caparison, generally excellent overall, contained in a generally very good second issue box. Sold for £60, Vectis, March.

Scarce Boxed Britains Set 7622 Swoppet Cowboys, wounded cowboy mounted, 632 throwing lasso mounted, 650 sheriff on foot, 651 bank robber on foot, 653 two gun cowboy and 654 with rifle standing firing, figures are in mint condition, window box, with vac insert, box has some age wear. Sold for £80, C&T Auctioneers, April.

Crescent Solids Wild West Range Canadian Tourist Board Issue Mounted RCMP, with 'Yukon Territory' standard, some minor paint loss, otherwise generally excellent overall, in a generally excellent illustrated box. Sold for £45, Vectis, March.

Britains Swoppets 15th Century Knights H.1450 Mounted Knight with Standard, mounted on a rearing brown horse, complete with blue blanket, generally excellent overall, in a generally very good second issue box. Sold for £80, Vectis, March.

Britains Cococubs Johnathan Boy, 1934, excellent condition. Sold for $225, Old Toy Soldier Auctions, May.

Timpo Arctic Series - The Arctic Display Set, including igloo, husky team with dogs, sledge, Eskimo, trappers, seals, polar bear, penguins and shrub section. Generally excellent. Sold for £120, Vectis, March.

Timpo Series 24 Hunters of the Frozen North, made 1973 to 1976, including sled with seal, baggage and equipment, dog sled team, hunters, walrus, polar bears and seals. Generally near mint. Sold for £25, Vectis, March.

Britains War Of Independence Bi-Centennial Anniversary Limited Edition Set no 5154 (1776-1976), six American Infantry, in mint boxed condition. Sold for £40, C&T Auctioneers, April.

Multiple Toymakers [New York] No. 435 Weird Monsters Set, 1964, mint, contained in a still sealed generally excellent shrink wrapped display card. Sold for £45, Vectis, July.

Introduction to...
Tinplate Toys

Tinplate is most certainly one of our favourite categories, thanks to the huge selection of large, brightly coloured vehicles, spaceships, robots and animals. It's hard not to love these fantastic vintage toys.

Although tinplate collections may not be as common as diecast models or toy locomotives, it's hard to deny that these often very large and colourful toys are some of the most attractive collectables around. What's more, they're a fantastic way to gauge the social themes of the period when they were produced, giving those historians among you a charming way to chart the rise and fall of particular interests.

Take, for example, the early 20th century when German companies like Marklin or Lehmann dominated the tinplate market. In those days it was replicas of cars and locomotives, which were then a very modern invention. As the century progressed and thoughts turned to a more militant theme then we start to see more tanks and planes appear. Once World War II was finished and production returned, then our thoughts drifted away from this planet and suddenly tinplate turned its attention to fantastic robots and space creatures. Sadly this later 'golden age' of tinplate production came around the same time as the more widespread use of cheaper plastic, so gradually tinplate was faded out in favour of this wonder material.

Still, the legacy left behind by tinplate is superb and the category caters for a wide range of tastes. Whether you like large scale replicas of famous cars, imaginative vehicles from other planets or intricate clockwork dioramas with numerous pieces, then it's likely you'll find a tinplate toy to match your tastes.

Arguably one of the most popular genres of tinplate is the fantastic range of robots produced in the 1960s by Japanese companies like Yonezawa or Horikawa. Although Japan was a relative latecomer to the tinplate scene, it quickly excelled in producing incredible brightly coloured androids. Some of these have become exceptionally

sought after with prices soaring into the tens of thousands for pieces like the Masudaya Radicon Robot, which sold for $37,000 in 2013! They're particularly popular in America too, as Japan imported a lot of its products to the States after World War II and auction houses like Bertoia and Morphy Auctions excel in selling rare examples.

What's more, it's not just the tinplate toys that are spectacular from the 1960s and many feature remarkable artwork on the box of the robots or spaceships inside – adding to their collectability and their display value.

However, that's not to say that tinplate isn't popular over here in the UK, it's just that our

prices tend to be a little more reserved when compared to our American counterparts. Also, we have a tendency to want the more established European makes, like Lehmann or Marklin as it's likely those are the toys that were more familiar on these shores. Although, that's not to say they were common - some of the large scale tinplate toys would have cost a small fortune at the time – particularly at the turn of the 20th century, so they weren't produced in huge numbers. Combine this with the fact that tinplate has a tendency to rust or the fact it's easily dented during frequent play sessions and you've got a recipe for high prices, as you'll notice in the pages ahead. ◾

149
Here you'll see almost 150 tinplate vehicles, spaceships, animals and robots.

19
The first tinplate toys appeared in the middle of the 19th century and were widely made until the 1960s.

£155
Not including some expensive robots, the average price is £155.

$9,500
As usual, the most expensive item was a Japanese robot. Read on to see which one!

£35,274
Our total hammer price for tinplate this year comes to £35,274.

Rise of the Robots

Rob Burman heads to the future with the intergalactic robots by Japanese maker Nomura

I don't know about you but after a childhood watching cartoons such as *The Jetsons* or science fiction series like *Star Trek*, I fully expected that by 2013 I would be flying to work in a hovercar and then arriving home to find my dinner cooked by a robotic maid. You can imagine my disappointment then to find myself currently coming to the office in a rusty Toyota Yaris and getting home only to discover my dinner in the fridge with a note from my wife telling me how long to put it in the microwave.

As such, it should probably come as no surprise to hear that I've had to get my robot fix in other ways, so thank goodness for the classic tinplate androids and spaceships from the 1950s and '60s. These incredibly curious and colourful toys evoke an age of wonder when inventors and designers were bravely stepping into a new world of scientific discovery. In particular, the Japanese manufacturers such as Nomura (also known as TN), Daiya, Modern Toys and Yoshiya produced some fantastic robots that have become incredibly collectable. Here, we'll revisit some of the more interesting items released by Nomura and cover a little bit of the company's intriguing history.

Although tinplate manufacture started in the mid-19th century, Japanese manufacturers didn't come into the fore until after World War II, when the production of tin toys resumed after being halted due to the need for raw materials. Under American occupation and the 'Marshall Plan', toy makers in Japan were granted the opportunity to resume manufacture, with the intention of giving the country all the low profit and high-labour manufacturing, while the United States would benefit from selling the imported product.

Nomura was one of the first companies in Japan to take advantage of this scheme and throughout the 1940s it became a dominant player in tinplate production. Its aim was to embody the new ideal of 'Wakon Yosai' – Japanese spirit, western technology – and with this idea in mind it began to produce robots, cars, spaceships and lots more. Specialising in mechanical and wind-up toys, Nomura was one of the biggest and most prolific of all post-war Japanese tinplate producers.

Part of the company's success was, in part, down to being in the right place at the right time. As Hollywood became obsessed with science fiction films during the Cold War, Nomura was perfectly placed to exploit this fascination with futuristic aliens and robots due to its range of brightly coloured toys. For example, one of Nomura's most recognisable and expensive robots is a battery-operated figure based on Robby the Robot from the 1956 film *Forbidden Planet*. Made in 1958, the toy features the recognisable see-through dome head and claw-like hands of the film version. Many consider this the 'holy grail' of robotic tinplate and a boxed toy in good condition can fetch more than £1,000. Interestingly at the start of the millennium Sotheby's in New York sold a version that had accidentally been given two left hands and it fetched well over the usual price, realising $11,400.

But it wasn't just the West that was falling in love with robots and back in Japan, many comic books began to tell fantastic stories of robotic characters such as Astro Boy and Tetsujin 28-go (also known as Gigantor in America). Once again, Nomura was in the right place to start producing toys based on the country's own homegrown talent. Tetsujin in particular, was a popular line for Nomura and the company produced several toys based on the robot, including the fairly standard wind-up figures but also some more intriguing items, like Tetsujin riding a tinplate motorbike, a train set and a 'flying' version that could be attached to a hook and would swing round. Perhaps the rarest of the range is Super Hero Tetsujin 28 No. 1, measuring seven inches high and made during the '60s. In fact, it's so rare, we struggled to find any recent auction results for it.

However, a number of Tetsujin models were recently

LEFT Batman inspired a huge range of collectables but none are quite as strange as this. When operated, the robot's head lights up and shuffles slowly along.

FAR LEFT The Robotank featured light up eyes and machine guns that popped out of his chest. We certainly wouldn't fancy going up against one of these on the battlefield!

One of the features that many Japanese robots share in common is a head that opens up to reveal a smaller, often grotesque, head inside.

part of a spectacular collection of tinplate/diecast robots sold by Morphy's Auctions in the USA. The most impressive was the SG-01 Tetsujin 28 Chogozoku, made by Japanese company Popy in 1981. It featured chrome detailing and glossy enameled parts. Standing almost 16 inches tall, the figure included armour panels that attached magnetically to an impressively detailed 'internal skeleton' to give it a 'beefed up' appearance. The left leg is also hollow and contains a

screw operated lift mechanism that can be used by tiny plastic crew figures. Estimated at $2,500 it realised a fantastic $4,200.

But it wasn't just space that was providing inspiration for Nomura and in 1966 the company produced a rather unusual cross between one of its more traditional robots and Adam West's iconic Batman. The result is a freaky third bat/third man/third robot walking figure complete with glowing head – the perfect thing to scare the villains of Gotham City.

Another unusual feature is that his feet look like they're turned backwards. Supposedly this is because the designers discovered that with the feet turned the correct way Batman tended to fall over, so they just flipped them round. A boxed Batman robot recently sold at Vectis Auctions in Thornaby for £1,500; proving there's still a lot of interest in this peculiar hybrid.

Well, we hope you've enjoyed this tour through tinplate. In many ways, we've only just

scratched the surface of the 'golden age' of Japanese space toys and there are several other manufacturers, including Daiya and Modern Toys, as well other items including UFOs, spaceships, futuristic vehicles and space guns. If this has tickled your fancy then there's plenty more to discover! ∎

BELOW Many Japanese robots featured unique functions. For example, this wonderful Tetsujin model can be attached to a hook on the ceiling, so it can fly around in circles.

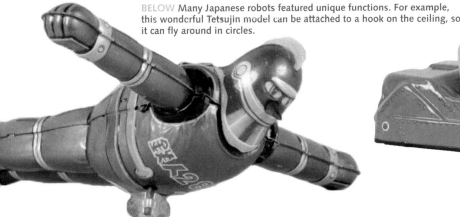

ABOVE Here you can see the Robby Space Patrol piece. Among collectors anything featuring the famous Forbidden Planet star is considered to be particularly collectable.

Robot Driving Tractor Toy, battery-operated, one of the more difficult versions to find, marked 'KO Japan'. Some minor scratching. Sold for $390, Morphy Auctions, September.

Schuco No.1085 Rollfix Mercedes 220S 2-door Car, near mint, 10.5"/16cm long and includes a good plus illustrated box. Sold for £700, Vectis, October.

Codeg (UK) Mechanical Space Shooting Range, very rare clockwork powered target range, made 1952/53. Excellent condition in a good card box. Sold for £320, Mullock's, October.

Schuco No.1085 Rollfix tinplate clockwork Mercedes Benz 220S, some small cracks to clear plastic rear windscreen otherwise excellent plus including a reproduction card box, 10.5"/27cm long. Sold for £360, Vectis, October.

Schuco No.5720 Electro Hydro-Car, includes steering wheel accessory, control cable and two wooden bollards, together with the instruction leaflet, 10"/26cm. Sold for £440, Vectis, October.

Sutcliffe 'Diana' tinplate clockwork cruiser, near mint, in working order with an excellent illustrated box. 12"/30cm long. Sold for £70, Vectis, October.

Schuco No.5509 Elektro Razzia Car, near mint, 9"/23cm long and comes with a fair illustrated card box with an end flap and an inner flap detached but present. Sold for £240, Vectis, October.

Friction Atom Robot, marked 'KO Japan', some oxidation to bare metal parts and moderate scratching throughout. Sold for $180, Morphy Auctions, September.

TN Toys (Japan) Space Gun, battery-operated with light ball end, in original illustrated box. Sold for £50, Mullock's, October.

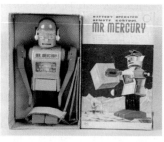

Remote Control Mr. Mercury Robot Toy, scarce box variation and robot is blue in colour. Marked 'Marx' on the front. Toy is excellent to near mint, box is very good to excellent. Sold for $840, Morphy Auctions, September.

Robot Bulldozer, scarce version with green litho, original box is included, with some staining to lid. Marked 'A Flare Product', 'Japan' and 'No. 115 United Pioneer Company'. Sold for $900, Morphy Auctions, September.

Technofix (Germany) No.303 'Cable Car' tinplate clockwork layout, some age wear but overall good plus to excellent, 18"/46cm long in a fair card box (end of box lid detached but present). Sold for £60, Vectis, October.

Schuco No.5308S 'Drivers School' Elektro Control Car, near mint in a good plus illustrated box with battery control box, steering wheel and cable accessory, two wooden bollards with road signs and correct Schuco screwdriver. Sold for £500, Vectis, October.

Remote Control Mr. Mercury Robot Toy, scarce box variation and robot is blue in colour. Marked 'Marx' on the front. Toy is excellent to near mint, box is very good to excellent. Sold for $840, Morphy Auctions, September.

Horikawa (Japan) Floating Satellite Mysterious Action Target Game, with tinplate gun and two rubber-tipped darts, plus two floating balls. In original box. Sold for £25, Mullock's, October.

Cragstan (Japan) Mr. Atomic Thinking Robot, excellent plus in a great card box with colourfully illustrated lid. Sold for £240, Mullock's, October.

Horikawa (Japan) Rotate-o-Matic Super Astronaut Robot, circa 1963, comes in an illustrated bodx with crushing to lid, clean battery box. Sold for £110, Mullock's, October.

DSK (Japan) Apollo II American Eagle Lunar Module, some light age wear but overall good plus to excellent in a fair illustrated box, 10"/25cm tall. Sold for £70, Vectis, October.

Modern Toys (Japan) M-99 Army Tank, near mint in a good illustrated box, 18"/45cm long. Sold for £90, Vectis, October.

Ball Playing Bear, battery-operated, includes original box with nice colour graphics. Condition is very good to excellent. Sold for $570, Morphy Auctions, September.

Yonezawa tinplate Golden Tiger Ack-Ack Tank, clean battery compartment. Excellent, 8.5"/21cm long in a fair card box. Sold for £70, Vectis, October.

Horikawa (Japan) Attacking Martian, comes in illustrated box with crushing to lid, clean battery box. Sold for £70, Mullock's, October.

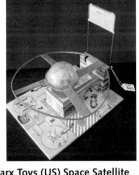

Marx Toys (US) Space Satellite Station, is in good working order, some slight damage to the plastic spinner. Sold for £40, Mullock's, October.

Battery powered Mobile Satellite Tracking Station, toy includes original box marked 'Cragstan' and 'Made by Yonezawa'. Near mint, old store stock. Sold for $1,020, Morphy Auctions, September.

Universe Boat, made in China, battery operated. Tinplate and plastic, includes all inserts in original box. Unused. Sold for $96, Morphy Auctions, September.

Sutcliffe Bluebird Clockwork Speed Boat, good plus, lacking key, in good box. Sold for £75, Aston's, September.

Milky Way Boat Spaceship, made in China, original box with inserts. Nice colourful original box. Near mint condition. Sold for $84, Morphy Auctions, September.

Tri-ang Minic No.60M Routemaster Bus, 'Tri-ang Pedal Motors' and 'Pengun' advertisements to sides, destination Putney. Length 17.5cm. Fair condition, decals overall good, paint loss and some corrosion particularly to lower body and base. Sold for £35, Aston's, September.

Nomura (Japan) Police Patrol Jeep, length 35cm, good condition, some corrosion to rear interior wheel arch. Sold for £80, Aston's, September.

Alps (Japan) Speed Challenger Battery Operated Race Car, good condition, clean battery compartment, some scratches, dents and corrosion to driver's helmet, in good box. Sold for £100, Aston's, September.

Universe Televiboat, made in China, battery operated, includes original box with graphics on lid. Sold for $120, Morphy Auctions, September.

Strange Explorer Space Tank, made by DSK, Japan. Tank rises up to reveal a gorilla creature. Sold for $150, Morphy Auctions, September.

Issmayer (Germany) tinplate and clockwork novelty chicken, tin printed detail in various colours, flapping wings and fixed key to rear, 18cm long. Sold for £65, Bamfords, October.

Space Patrol, made by Modern Toys, includes original box with inserts. Box has some creasing and wear, which the toy has very little wear. Condition is very good to excellent. Sold for $480, Morphy Auctions, September.

Marusan Toys (Japan) SAN tinplate and clockwork novelty walking and crying swan, wearing a black top hat, flapping wings, moving feet and fixed key to side, 16cm high, boxed. Sold for £50, Bamfords, October.

Wind-up Jupiter Space Craft, some oxidation to metal ring around the dome, plus scratching and wear. Box marked 'K Made in Japan'. Condition is very good to excellent/ Sold for $150, Morphy Auctions, September.

Hans Eberl (Germany) tinplate and clockwork Ebo Pao-Pao Peacock, lithographed tin printed and painted detail, fixed key mechanism to tail, 24cm long, c.1920. Sold for £110, Bamfords, October.

Tinplate Space Tank, made in China, original box with colourful graphics. Original box includes inserts. Sold for $150, Morphy Auctions, September.

Yonezawa (Japan) Jet Speed Racer, good condition, some spots of corrosion to base and around battery compartment cover but clean battery compartment. Sold for £100, Aston's, September.

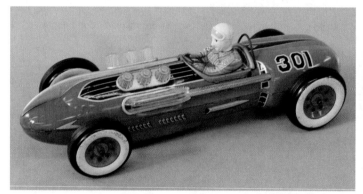

Masudaya (Japan) Racing Car, fair condition, missing windscreen. Sold for £85, Aston's, September.

Piston Robot, marked 'SH Japan', toy is old store stock with very little to no wear. Excellent to mint condition, box very good to excellent. Sold for $720, Morphy Auctions, September.

DIECAST   RAILWAYS   TOY FIGURES   TINPLATE   TV & FILM   OTHERS   EBUYS

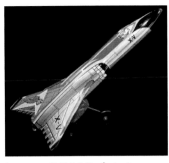

Japanese X-V Jet Rocket, circa 1960s, made by Yone, push down with wind-up action. Sold for $240, Morphy Auctions, September.

Lehmann (Germany) 645 tinplate and clockwork novelty PAAK-PAAK QUACK-QUACK toy, lithographed tin printed detail, fixed key to side, 19cm long. Sold for £120, Bamfords, October.

Mechanical Moon Creature, includes original box showing moon creature on space planet. Marked 'Made in Japan' and 'Marx'. Minor scratching and wear. Sold for $270, Morphy Auctions, September.

Louis Marx Uncle Wiggly Car, in original tatty box, toy is in excellent condition. Sold for $501.50, Bertoia Auctions, September.

Space Jet vehicle, toy is marked 'X-001' on top and 'Bandai Made in Japan' on the bottom. Slight oxidation to battery box and bare metal parts, plus scratching to lid. Sold for $420, Morphy Auctions, September.

Louis Marx New York City Toy, very good to exclusive conition. Sold for $118, Bertoia Auctions, September.

Explorer Space Tank, includes very colourful and crisp original box, marked 'Cragstan'. Near mint, old store stock. Sold for $540, Morphy Auctions, September.

Cragstan Space Mobile, box is complete but does have some staining and tearing. Very good condition. Sold for $660, Morphy Auctions, September.

JML (France) No.0158 tinplate clockwork motorcycle, some age wear, headlamp lacks its lens otherwise good, 12"/30cm. Sold for £220, Vectis, December.

Marx Cowboy Rider, brown horse version, pristine condition. Sold for $295, Bertoia Auctions, September.

Japanese Tin Space Capsule, circa 1963, made by SH Horikawa. Metal hinges scuffed. Near mint condition. Sold for $240, Morphy Auctions, September.

USA Nasa Gemini X5, 3414 Masudaya Japan circa 1966, in very good untested condition, some tarnish to chrome, with an excellent original box with inner packing. Sold for £95, C&T Auctions, October.

SH Horikawa Japan New Space Capsule, circa 1960s, in good untested condition, with internal packing, box has age wear, water staining. Sold for £80, C&T Auctions, October.

SH Horikawa Japan New Space Capsule, circa 1960s, in near mint untested condition, with internal packing, box has some age wear. Sold for £130, C&T Auctions, October.

Friendship Space Capsule S.H. Horikawa Japan, circa 1960s, in very good condition, box is fair to good, with some age wear and repairs. Sold for £95, C&T Auctions, October.

Schuco Bavarian Tyrolean Seppi, cloth covered tinplate, wind-up dancing figure with violin. Sold for £80, Reeman Dansie, December.

Machine Robot SH Horikawa Japan, circa 1960s, some slight rust to battery compartment, in good untested condition, with internal packing, box is good, with some age wear, still displays well! Sold for £220, C&T Auctions, October.

Schuco Arcobat Bear, cloth covered tinplate wind-up figure of bear with red shorts and mouse with raffia skirt. Sold for £90, Reeman Dansie, December.

Schuco Arcobatic Kangaroo and Joey, cloth covered tinplate wind-up figure. Sold for £70, Reeman Dansie, December.

Alps (Japan) large tinplate Police Department Motorcycle, battery compartment cover at base is loose but present, registration number PD0248, with battery operated lamps to front and rear, rubber tyres, some play wear but overall a good impressive example for display. Sold for £220, Vectis, December.

Wells Brimtoy Pocketoy tinplate friction drive London style Double Decker Bus, circa 1950s, red with tinprinted detail including driver and conductor. Good plus, 4.5"/11cm long. Sold for £35, Vectis, December.

Arnold (Germany) No.A643 tinplate clockwork motorcycle, clockwork motor to rear wheels in working order and includes the red headlamp lens, 20cm/8" long. Good plus. Sold for £240, Vectis, December.

Schuco Monk with stein, cloth covered tinplate, wind-up dancing figure. Sold for £90, Reeman Dansie, December.

Asahi Toy Japan XZ-7 Space Ship, in excellent original condition, with a fair original box. Sold for £50, C&T Auctions, October.

Mettoy (UK) tinplate clockwork AA Motorcycle and Sidecar, diecast spoked wheels, JLX 500 registration number, requires a male key, 3.5"/9cm. Good plus. Sold for £80, Vectis, December.

Baron tinplate clockwork No. 540 car, finished in blue, cream and red, with driver and passenger, length approx 33cm, boxed (box lightly creased and scuffed). Sold for £95, Toovey's, December.

Masudaya Japan Apollo Spacecraft, in excellent untested condition, with internal packing, box is very good, some slight age wear. Sold for £190, C&T Auctions, October.

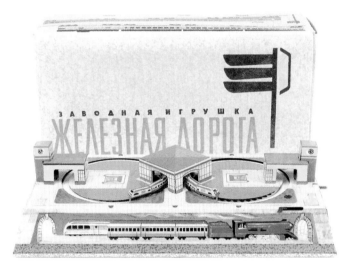

Eastern European tinplate clockwork Train Set, detailed tinprinting, working order with key and brake, 10"/24cm long. Sold for £10, Vectis, December.

Schuco tinplate No. 5311 Elektro Ingenico car, finished in red, length approx 21cm, boxed, with controller, traffic signs, etc (playwear and scratch marks, box creased, torn and scuffed). Sold for £90, Toovey's, December.

Nomura Japan Moon Traveller Apollo-Z, in good original untested condition, radar antenna is broken, with internal packing pieces in a very good original box. Sold for £45, C&T Auctions, October.

SH Horikawa Japan Video Robot, in excellent boxed untested condition with internal packing, box has slight age wear. Sold for £65, C&T Auctions, October.

SH Horikawa Japan Missile Robot With Missile Shooting Action, in mint boxed untested condition with all internal packing. Sold for £82, C&T Auctions, October.

SH Horikawa Japan Space Patrol Robot, in near mint untested condition with a fair to good original box, some repairs Sold for £150, C&T Auctions, October.

Masudaya Japan US Apollo Project, in near mint untested condition, with a very good original box (some creasing to lid). Sold for £110, C&T Auctions, October.

Nomura TN Toys Japan Solar X-8 Nasa Space Rocket, in near mint untested condition with a good original box, some slight age wear. Sold for £80, C&T Auctions, October.

SH Horikawa Japan Rotate-O-Matic Super Astronaut Robot, in near mint untested condition with a very good original box. Sold for £100, C&T Auctions, October.

Wells clockwork monoplane, registration G-E OBT, 27cm, good to fair condition. Sold for £50, Tennants, December.

Horikawa Japan Piston Robot, in mint boxed untested condition with internal packing. Sold for £150, C&T Auctions, October.

Super Robot (Apollo 2000) SH Horikawa Japan, in near mint untested condition with a fair original box, one corner of lid split. Sold for £130, C&T Auctions, October.

SH Horikawa Japan Fighting Space Man Robot, in near mint untested condition, internal packing, with a very good original box, with one corner of lid repaired. Sold for £350, C&T Auctions, October.

SH Horikawa Japan Rotate-O-Matic Super Astronaut Robot, in near mint untested condition, internal packing, with a very good original box. Sold for £130, C&T Auctions, October.

Space Saucer Mercury X-1 Item No. 750 Yonezawa for Mego, in near mint untested condition, with a very good box. Sold for £85, C&T Auctions, October.

SH Horikawa Japan Secret Weapon Space Scout Robot, in very good untested condition with a fair to good original box, one split to corner of lid. Sold for £230, C&T Auctions, October.

Cragstan Satellite Outer Space Survey Ship X-07, in very good untested condition, with internal packing, box is excellent, with some slight age wear. Sold for £130, C&T Auctions, October.

Nomura TN Toys Japan Solar X-7 Space Rocket, inner packing in near mint untested condition with a good original box, some slight age wear. Sold for £75, C&T Auctions, October.

DIECAST | RAILWAYS | TOY FIGURES | TINPLATE | TV & FILM | OTHERS | EBUYS

Action Clockwork Planet Robot, KO Toys Yoshiya Japan, tarnishing to chrome plated parts, in good working condition, complete with original illustrated box, with some age wear. Sold for £160, C&T Auctions, October.

Yonezawa Japan battery operated talking robot, light wear and losses to raised edges, some areas of rusting, battery boxed damaged with battery cover missing Sold for £90, Lacy, Scott & Knight, November.

German tinplate and clockwork snapping floor crocodile, lithographed body with fixed key mechanism, when wound the mechanism powers a snapping jaw, marked 'Made in Germany'. Sold for £30, Lacy, Scott & Knight, November.

Lehmann 1903 Tut-Tut wind-up toy, marked - Deutsch Voran Lehmann Tut Tut D R Patente Engl Patents. BTS S.G.D.G. Frame PAT USA May 12 1903 (horn still working). Sold for £230, Reeman Dansie, December.

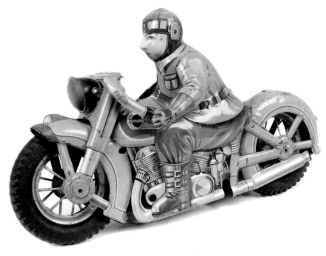

Yonezawa 1950s Harley tinplate motorcycle, lacks the mechanism but does include spokes, wheels and rubber tyres, fair to good for display, 15"/39cm. Sold for £240, Vectis, December.

Schuco Akustico 2002 Car, no windscreen, some scratching to underside otherwise good. Sold for £25, Lacy, Scott & Knight, November.

Wells Brimtoy Pocketoy tinplate Trolleybus, tinprinted detail including driver and conductor, some wear to edges and trolley poles but overall a good plus bright example. Sold for £45, Vectis, December.

Taiyo (Japan) Battery Operated Mystery Action Fire Chief Car, white/red with red roof light 10.5", 27cm, excellent, box good to excellent. Sold for £50, Tennants, December.

Streamline Electric Sedan, of unknown manufacture but probably Japanese, battery compartment to underside, in the original illustrated lift-off lid box. Sold for £100, Lacy, Scott & Knight, November.

S.H. Horikawa Japan Battery Operated Fighting Robot, one hinge broken on rear battery door, in good condition, with internal packing, box is good, with some age wear, still displays well. Sold for £180, C&T Auctions, October.

Pre-War Tinplate and Lithographed Model of a "Konsum" Aircraft, possibly a toy biscuit tin for a Swedish Cooperative Type Store. Good condition. Sold for £280, Lacy, Scott & Knight, November.

SH Horikawa Japan New Space Capsule, rare green body, orange plastic lens to top, opening front hatch to reveal astronaut with camera, in very good untested condition, with internal packing, box is excellent. Sold for £130, C&T Auctions, October.

German friction driven twin funnel steamer, red, green and white livery. Sold for £100, Reeman Dansie, December.

Sutcliffe Models tinplate clockwork Sea Wolf Submarine, with plastic fittings, lacks key but includes rubber bung and periscope, propeller and rudder, working order. Excellent in a fair card box. Sold for £50, Vectis, December.

Philip Neidermeier (PN Germany) large tinplate Police Car, some light play wear, but otherwise a good plus to excellent bright example, 10.5"/26cm long and comes in a good illustrated box. Sold for £120, Vectis, February.

Technofix (Germany) No.282 tinplate friction drive Scooter, circa 1950s, with tin printed rider and lady pillion passenger, lacks windscreen, otherwise good. Sold for £130, Vectis, February.

Schuco No.1000 Curvo tinplate clockwork Motorcycle, red, with tinprinted detail including rider wearing a green shirt, clockwork motor in working order. Good plus to excellent for display, with original Schuco key. Sold for £100, Vectis, February.

Tipp & Co (Germany) No.598 1950s friction driver motorcycle, some surface corrosion to part of the front balloon wheel and lacks the clear plastic windscreen, complete with both panniers and rear mounted registration number TCO-598, 122mm/30cm long. Fair to good. Sold for £140, Vectis, December.

Marx Toys (USA) tinplate clockwork Police Motorcycle with Siren, yellow, with tin printed detail, motor and siren in working order, 85"/22cm - good plus. Sold for £110, Vectis, February.

K Toys (Japan) Police Motorcycle, white, with tinprinted detail including blue uniformed rider, rubber tyre to front wheel, clockwork spring requires attention, 7"/18cm. Good plus. Sold for £70, Vectis, February.

Technofix No.GE255 tinplate clockwork Racing Motorcycle, orange, including rider, racing number two, in working order, an excellent example from the period of French manufacture, 7"/18cm. Sold for £50, Vectis, February.

Mettoy (UK) No.2613840 Military Motorcycle, tinplate example, green with tin printed detail including rider, friction drive, some age wear but overall good for display, 6"/15cm. Sold for £90, Vectis, February.

Tipp & Co (Germany) No.59 "Silver Racer" novelty Motorcycle and Sidecar, scarce 1950s example, silver with tin printed detail including rider and pillion passenger, clockwork motor in working order, side to side movement of front wheel is connected to the sidecar passenger who leans out on corners and returns to a seated position (requires some adjustment), with working brake, 7"/18cm. Good plus example. Sold for £400, Vectis, February.

Schuco No.4520 "Flic" clockwork Traffic Policeman figure, scarce example with grey tinplate base, with 4-faced warning signals and operating brake. Excellent plus in box with illustrated lid, packaging and original "Schuco" key. Sold for £120, Vectis, February.

Marx Toys (Japan) "Mr. Mercury", a scarce example with red feet and hat, clear plastic visor, open chest, bronze body, grey legs and arms, broken plastic battery casing but robot includes both white plastic ears, battery control cable is attached (broken control box fastening). Good for display, 13"/33cm high. Sold for £140, Vectis, February.

Schuco No.500 Magico Garage, tinplate structure, brown corrugated roof, brick effect and turquoise opening doors, telephone accessory to side. Excellent plus in excellent illustrated box - rare in this condition. Sold for £40, Vectis, February.

JNF (Germany) Silberpfeil Mercedes Racing Car, beige, friction drive car with steerable front wheels, some small scratches and missing screen but overall good plus in illustrated card box which lacks an end flap but is otherwise fair. Sold for £100, Vectis, February.

Flying Saucer Roundabout, of unconfirmed manufacture, marked "Foreign", in working order with brake, detail tinprinting with four revolving cars. Good plus, 9.5"/24cm in diameter. Sold for £70, Vectis, February.

Wells (UK) pre-war "National Service" tinplate clockwork bus, scarce example in red with tinprinted detail including passengers and driver, 1934 registration plate, blue wheels, motor in working order, some age wear but generally good overall, 7"/18cm long. Sold for £60, Vectis, February.

Modern Toys (Japan) "Remote Control Sports Car", in working order but the mechanical steering control requires repair otherwise good plus for display in a good illustrated box. Sold for £80, Vectis, February.

SSS (Japan) large tinplate Power Shovel on Diesel Truck, in working order. Good plus, in a good illustrated box, 14"/35cm. Sold for £140, Vectis, February.

K Toys (Japan) tinplate "Bread and Cake" Bakers Delivery Van, tinprinted detail with friction motor and chef lithographed on roof. Excellent, 4"/10cm long. Sold for £40, Vectis, February.

Schuco Elektro Radiant 5600 BOAC Aircraft, some discolouration to model, battery box is clean, 48cm, with original repaired box and instruction leaflet. Sold for £190, Lacy, Scott & Knight, February.

Marusan (Japan) 1957 tinplate friction drive Police Car, black/white, slight scuffs to lower edges of driver's side, otherwise excellent bright example, 5"/13cm which still retains a good plus card box with illustrated lid. Sold for £45, Vectis, February.

Schuco No.2095 Mercedes Benz 190SL Open Top, scarce colour variation is green, with red plastic interior, clockwork motor to rear wheels, in working order with correct Schuco key, some slight discolouration to the driver's side paintwork and small corrosion mark above rear wheel arch otherwise good plus. Sold for £120, Vectis, February.

Lehmann 651 EPL·1 clockwork lithographed tinplate Airship, with original plastic propeller blades, in original box, very good, clockwork tested well at time of cataloguing, box passable, lid lacks four sides. Sold for £210, Special Auction Services, March.

Chad Valley (UK) tinplate Mobile Snack Bar, clockwork motor in working order with key, light play wear but overall good plus. Sold for £40, Vectis, February.

Mettoy Tinplate Clockwork Car, plated parts have faded and corrosion/playwear to edges, otherwise good, rear spare wheel missing. Sold for £65, Lacy, Scott & Knight, February.

Wells Tinplate and Clockwork Tipping Lorry, fixed single key mechanism in working order, some re-glueing to underside of tipper, good condition. Sold for £60, Lacy, Scott & Knight, February.

Ichiko Japan 'You Can Ride Em' Mercedes-Benz 300SE, large scale tinplate Mercedes in red with hard plastic wheels, chromed bumpers and tinprinted interior, 610mm in length, in original box, excellent, box good. Sold for £130, Special Auction Services, March.

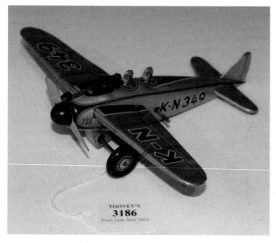

Tinplate Clockwork Two Seat Monoplane, possibly by Kellerman, serial No. K-N349, some playwear. Sold for £100, Toovey's, March.

Mettoy Tinplate Clockwork Car, with rear spare wheel, noticeable playwear and fadedto plated parts. Sold for £70, Lacy, Scott & Knight, February.

Wells Tinplate and Clockwork Breakdown Service Lorry, scarce issue, model has areas of corrosion and paint losses, fair to good. Sold for £75, Lacy, Scott & Knight, February.

Mettoy Tinplate Clockwork Car & Caravan Set, two-door sedan in blue and cream with clockwork motor, caravan in cream with red detailing and sliding roof, marked TMC9595, contained in original plain card box marked 3023T, very good, box fair. Sold for £130, Special Auction Services, March.

Lemezaru Gyar 'Holdraketa Rocket', in working order with original box and instruction leaflet, some losses. Sold for £45, Lacy, Scott & Knight, February.

Horikawa (SH) Japan Swivel-O-Matic Astronaut Robot, brown tinplate battery operated robot with human face behind plastic visor, tinplate arms, red plastic feet, 1960s-70s issue, good to very good. Sold for £80, Special Auction Services, March.

Bing Tinplate Clockwork Four-Seater Open Tourer, fair, back panel resprayed, one wheel replaced, one repaired, retouching to windscreen, driver restored. Sold for £420, Special Auction Services, March.

Nomura (TN) Japan Fire Command Car, battery-operated tinplate Jeep with red body, black chassis, tin firemen figures, one steering, one with receiver and rubber tyres with tinplate hubs, in original box, very good, driver with hand loose from steering wheel, box fair to good. Sold for £110, Special Auction Services, March.

Nomura (TN) Japan Sports Car Skyliner, battery-operated tinplate car with red body, white roof, rubber tyres with tinplate 'Ford' hubs, in original box, very good, box fair. Sold for £85, Special Auction Services, March.

JNF Germany Mercedes Monoposto Racing Car, large tinplate friction powered car, red body, tinprinted cockpit, racing number four, in original box, good, lacks driver and windscreen, box passable. Sold for £110, Special Auction Services, March.

DIECAST   RAILWAYS   TOY FIGURES   TINPLATE   TV & FILM   OTHERS   EBUYS

Chad Valley Tinplate Climbing Miller, similar to Lehmann version, comprising windmill, miller figure and weighted sack, with original box lid, good to very good, lid passable to fair. Sold for £50, Special Auction Services, March.

Yonezawa (Japan) Cragstan Crapshooter, battery-operated toy with vinyl faced figure, tinplate base with felt lined table and tinprinted detailing, in original box with three die, very good, battery compartment clean, box passable to fair. Sold for £35, Special Auction Services, March.

Yonezawa Cragstan Robot, scarce colour and box variation, minor scratching and wear. Box has slight creasing. Sold for $1,200, Morphy Auctions, May.

Yonezawa Space Man, does have some edge wear and creasing on box, minor rubbing and wear on robot. Sold for $3,500, Morphy Auctions, May.

Chad Valley National Single Decker bus, with 'London De Luxe Express Glasgow' on side, good, clockwork not working. Sold for £100, Special Auction Services, July.

CIJ Citroen 'Petite Rosalie', very good, scratch to one side. Sold for £120, Special Auction Services, July.

Wells Brimtoy clockwork Racing Car, circa 1951, 30cm long with permanent key and working motor, some light overall wear. Replacement screen and rear aerofoil. Sold for £40, Vectis, July.

Lehmann ALSO 700 clockwork car, good to very good condition. Sold for £160, Special Auction Services, July.

Yonezawa Directional Robot, minor scratching and wear, minor creasing to box. Sold for $2,250, Morphy Auctions, May.

Aoshin Shoten Mechanical Chime Trooper, toy works and chimes, excellent condition, box very good to excellent. Sold for $9,500, Morphy Auctions, May.

Yoshiya Moon Explorer, robot has minimal wear, box very good to excellent. Sold for $2,250, Morphy Auctions, May.

Yonezawa Roby Robot, robot has one scratch on upper right arm, slight scratching to back. Sold for $2,000, Morphy Auctions, May.

DIECAST   RAILWAYS   TOY FIGURES   TINPLATE   TV & FILM   OTHERS   EBUYS

Introduction to...
TV & Film

From iconic vehicles like the Starship Enterprise, pictured here, to characters from *Star Wars*, TV & film memorabilia is an increasingly popular theme for collectors.

Once again it's been a good year for TV and film collectables, with several auctioneers such as East Bristol Auctions really looking to expand their TV and film offerings with more 'modern' items from the 1980s, such as *Ghostbusters* and *Transformers*, while established salerooms like Vectis continue to achieve incredible results for *Star Wars* action figures.

Although some have predicted the bubble must eventually burst for mint in box *Star Wars* figures, it doesn't appear to have happened yet and hardcore collectors around the world will still pay top whack for exceptional pieces. It doesn't necessarily matter if they're particularly rare, it's the quality that they're after. The most sought after items are those made by Palitoy for the original film in the late 1970s, as these weren't produced in huge numbers (unlike Kenner).

Then, of course, you've got the *Force Awakens* effect as the media builds up to the release of the new film in December. Thus people are bound to remember the original movies and this bump in nostalgia is likely to lead

to an increased interest in the toys too. With some auctioneers regularly reporting there isn't enough Palitoy stock to satisfy demand already, then this boost in awareness will potentially increase demand even more, meaning 2016 could be a bumper year for Star Wars at auction.

Meanwhile, for those who prefer their TV and film collectables with a little more vintage, then 2015 has seen some significant milestones, such as the 50th anniversary of Gerry Anderson's *Thunderbirds*. Once again, key anniversaries like this ensure there's more media

coverage for the original series and this interest also provides a potential spike in auction prices.

Arguably one of the most encouraging aspects of TV and film collectables is that they're inspiring a younger generation to become interested in collecting. Although they may initially start by just buying Batman items, by going to auctions or toy fairs, they're more than likely to see something else that grabs their attention and suddenly their collecting habits may change.

It's also a category where many of the prices – apart from, perhaps, *Star Wars* – haven't necessarily

reached their peak as members of the general public may not realise that toys from the 1980s or even the 1990s are now considered 'collectable' by certain groups who are willing to pay hard cash for them. Take, for example, East Bristol Auctions who took a large collection of boxed *Ghostbusters* toys from a vendor who was close to throwing them out. As a result, there's still an opportunity to pick up 'collectables of the future' like this from charity shops, car boots and even toy fairs because the seller may consider them to be 'worthless' compared to diecast cars or model railways. ∎

175 You'll find more than 170 toys listed in the TV and film section.

$5 That's actually $5 billion, as Disney is predicting that *Star Wars Force Awakens* toy sales could exceed $5 billion!

£155 Our average price is £155 - slightly up on last year's £146.

£1,300 This year's most expensive item was a Fortress Maximus Transformer.

£27,213 In total there is £27,213 worth of vintage toys in this section.

75 years of Batman

Don your Batman costume to celebrate the Caped Crusader's recent anniversary and remember some of the more unusual crime busting toys.

n May 1939 one of the most iconic figures of 20th century popular culture was born, inspiring a host of comics, movies, TV shows, novels, videogames... in fact, you name it and it's likely you'll see the distinctive mark of this legendary character. The individual in question is Batman, who certainly doesn't look bad for a 75-year-old. Since being introduced in the '30s Batman has gone on to inspire a whole host of toys – from diecast models to boardgames, costumes and lots more. To celebrate his recent birthday, we're taking a look at the origins of the Caped Crusader before remembering some of the more uncommon toys that bear his image.

The 1930s and '40s were arguably the golden age of comic books, with characters like Superman and Captain America all introduced during the period. It was the arrival of Superman in 1938 that really kicked things off and his appearance in *Action Comics #1* turned comics into a major (and lucrative) industry. Inspired by the man in tights, National Publications (the precursor to DC Comics) wanted to produce its own superhero and so Bob Kane, comic book writer and artist, came up with a character called "the Bat-Man".

Interestingly, the initial concept didn't look much like the Batman we know today. Originally he resembled Superman, with red tights and boots, no gloves, no gauntlet and wore a small 'domino mask'. He also had two stiff bat wings that stuck out from the outfit. Thankfully, Kane's fellow collaborator Bill Finger put the finishes touches to the design, suggesting that he wore a grey

ABOVE
ASC Asohin Batmobile. All models courtesy of Jim "Mr Star Wars" Stevenson.

outfit to be more ominous, while the wings – which could be cumbersome during a fight – were replaced with a cape, sculpted to look like bat wings.

In terms of his personality, Kane and Finger looked at popular culture of the period, in particular pulp fiction detective stories, along with fictional characters, like the Scarlet Pimpernel, Zorro and Dick Tracey. Even Sherlock Holmes had a look in because Batman was originally a master detective, rather than a superhero.

The first Batman story – *The Case of the Chemical Syndicate* – appeared in *Detective Comics #27*. Originally Detective Comics featured a number of different strips, along with stories featuring hard-boiled detectives but by January 1940, Batman had become the main cover star. One of the biggest changes for Batman came

in the 1960s with the launch of the television series in 1996, which saw circulation of the comics reach almost 900,000. Although the show only lasted until 1968 it produced some of the most iconic representations of Batman, including the Batmobile and the costume worn by Adam West. It also saw the development of some of the best Batman-related toys.

ASC ASOHIN BATMOBILE

Released in conjunction with the television series, Japanese company ASC/Asohin continued to release a superb tinplate Batmobile into the early 1970s. There are four variations of the model available and each comes in a slightly different box. The earliest example comes with the ASC logo on the box, while the later varieties ditch this in favour of Asohin. The model itself is a

super replica of the iconic vehicle, complete with Batman and Robin behind the wheel. Along with a more realistic black version, Asohin also made blue, red and silver Batmobiles. However, it's the original that's the most sought after with a price tag of around £800.

FAIRYLITE BATMAN ROBOT

Fairylite is perhaps best known for the large Batman robot made by Japanese company Nomura but released over here under the Fairylite name. However, it also produced a more unusual Batman Robot that has a wind-up action. It terms of appearance it looks like the larger Nomura robot has been crushed in one of the Joker's deadly traps and is rather squashed, compared to its cousin. The two robots even use the same box art – showing Batman leaping

Elderly relatives and delicate China dinner services beware because little Timmy has just got the Baravelli Batman Rocket Gun for Christmas. Bash, bang, ka-pow!

The Joker's latest evil scheme sees Batman squashed inside a giant lemon squeezer... at least that's what it looks like with the Fairylite wind-up Batman Robot.

Batman's image is so iconic that even basic pictures of the superhero can add visual value to the simplest of products, like this basic Batmask.

Mego's World's Greatest Superheroes range includes some of the best action figures based on Batman and Robin. Plus, you can even pick up replicas of the Batmobile and Wayne Manor big enough to fit the figures inside. Definitely among our favourite classic Batman toys.

BELOW
The result of unholy relations between a Dalek and Bruce Wayne, with this creepy and weird-looking Batcraft from Marx Toys. Is it a hovercraft? Is it a car? Is it worth anything?!

towards a rope ladder, while Robin sits in the Batmobile. This charming little figure should set you back around £700, in good condition.

MEGO WORLD'S GREATEST SUPERHEROES

Mego created a large range of action figures based on comic characters, as part of its brilliant World's Greatest Superheroes range. Iron Man, Superman, Aquaman and more all made appearances in the series but the ones that kicked it all off were, you guessed it, Batman and Robin. The Dynamic Duo continued to appear in the World's Greatest Superheroes range for several years but it's the two models originally released in 1973 that command the big money. That's because Batman has a removeable cowl, while Robin's eyemask can

be removed – later variations removed this optional extra and the head had the masks moulded on. Even better is the Batman with removeable cowl that comes in a solid box, rather than the more common window box... if you have one of these, then you're sitting on a very rare piece.

As well as introducing figures, Mego also launched a range of superb vehicles based on the Batman comics/television series. Of course, the all-important Batmobile was available but Mego also released more unusual items, like the Jokermobile, which is basically a bright green VW Microbus covered in stickers proclaiming "ha-ha" or "hoooo". However, the best accessory from Mego is definitely the large-scale Wayne Foundation, which is actually Mego's take on the Batcave. This four-floor structure has Wayne Manor on the top level,

while a secret lift can transport action figures to the Bat Cave below. The project was designed by DC Comics and you can certainly tell, thanks to the wonderful attention to detail in the artwork, which features cameos from little known Batman characters, like Bat-Mite. Incredibly the box on its own for the Wayne Foundation recently sold for eBay for around £200!

BARAVELLI BATMAN ROCKET GUN

Made by Italian company Baravelli in 1966 for the British market, the Batman Rocket Gun measures 22-inches and can be used to fire two 6-inch rockets. The battery-operated gun produces sound effects and has a dual-firing action, thanks to two trigger mechanisms. The box has a gorgeous illustration of Batman blasting away with the weapon...

despite the fact that in the comics he makes a solemn vow never to kill anyone. There are at least two variations of the Rocket Gun available and it comes in red and blue. A red version sold at auction in America last year for $862.

MARX TOYS BATCRAFT

From the sublime to the ridiculous now with the Marx Toys Batcraft from 1966, as made by the Swansea-based toy manufacturer. This battery-operated vehicle looks like a weird mix of hovercraft, helicopter and Dalek, with lights on the top and front. It also had the famous 'mystery action' movement that was so common in battery-operated toys of the '60s. We can't really imagine Batman zipping around in this in the comics but at least the box art makes this bizarre vehicle look cool. ■

Playset pleasures

Travelling to a galaxy far, far away to remember some of the classic Star Wars playsets from Kenner and Palitoy.

A long time ago in a galaxy far, far away (well, Grimsby in the 1980s, which arguably may as well have been a different planet to the rest of the UK) there was only one thing on my mind – Star Wars! After seeing the original film, my mind had been blown by the adventures of Luke Skywalker and his efforts to bring down the evil Empire. Everything in my bedroom was Star Wars themed, from the bed sheets to the curtains and probably even my underpants. But, of course, my favourite items were the wonderful toys created by Palitoy and also Kenner, with some of the greatest being the fantastic playsets by both companies. Here, we'll take a look at some of the best and compare the differences between the two manufacturers.

Well, let's kick things off in style with one of the best and now hardest to find playsets – the Palitoy Death Star, which was originally only available in the UK, Australia and Canada. Released in 1977 the Emperor's infamous planet destroying super weapon is recreated in cardboard. The large semi-sphere (approx. 60cm in diameter) was big enough to fit action figures inside and featured some wonderful illustrations of key locations from the film, such as the trash compactor, cell block, command centre and rotating gun placement. This impressive beast was held together with 10 plastic clips and also included six special bases for mounting action figures on. Due to its cardboard construction, tracking one down in mint condition nowadays is no easy feat and even spare parts regularly trade for decent prices (particularly in America where

ABOVE
You will never find a more wretched hive of scum and villainy, replicated in toy form.

LEFT
That's no moon... it's a space station made of cardboard and little bits of plastic.

the set was never released). Interestingly, Australian toy maker Toltoys made an almost identical Death Star but instead of being made of cardboard, it was recreated in much sturdier chipboard.

Meanwhile in America, Kenner's take on the Death Star was totally different and instead of being a cardboard sphere, it was more like a plastic tower with card walls. Kenner's Death Star was the largest and first playset released by the company and had

lots of interesting features, such as an elevator that travelled to the different floors, laser cannon and the opportunity to recreate the dramatic 'bridge scene' by swinging Luke and Princess Leia over the retracting drawbridge.

If you fancied a more relaxed adventure, then the Palitoy Cantina could have been the thing for you. The Cantina is shown in the first Star Wars film and is the location where Luke first meets smuggler Han Solo. It's a bit of a dodgy dive full of weird aliens and

unusual characters (please, no mentions of Grimsby again). The playset recreated this nicely, with a cool card backdrop depicting the strange drinkers while the plastic base had a sunken 'bar area' where your various action figures could stop for a quick pint of Bantha Brew. There was also a cool 'battle action' function that allowed Obi Wan Kenobi to whack Greedo the alien in the face with just the press of a button.

Once again, over in America Kenner had a slightly different

Look at the lack of excitement on that child's face... he's wondering why he didn't get the Palitoy Death Star for Christmas.

RIGHT
Until this battle station is fully operational, it is vulnerable... vulnerable to getting knocked over by enthusiastic children desperate to use the slightly wobbly lift.

Just remember to apologise about the mess if you kill any alien bounty hunters while playing with the Palitoy Cantina playset.

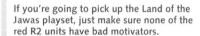

If you're going to pick up the Land of the Jawas playset, just make sure none of the red R2 units have bad motivators.

ABOVE
Build your own Astromech, just like R2-D2, with the Palitoy Droid Factoy.

ABOVE
This isn't the droid factory you're looking for... it's much better to pick up the Palitoy version.

take on the Cantina. Although the card backdrop was the same, the base was different, which gave the playset some new features, including an opening Cantina door, a mock battle scene between Han Solo and Greedo and a slightly different battle action for Obi Wan at the bar. Kenner's is probably the better playset thanks to the more interesting action features.

On the subject of differences – one of the playsets with the most obvious differences between Palitoy and Kenner was the Droid Factory. In fact, the only real resemblance between the two is the name. In the UK Palitoy created a factory with a conveyor belt to transport the various droid parts through the different locations within the imaginary factory. The playset did actually come with droid parts to allow you to build the little robots yourself.

For completists, it's worth noting Palitoy produced a version with a yellow plastic base and also a blue one.

Meanwhile, across the Pond, Kenner decided its Droid Factory would use a crane to carry the robot parts around, rather than a conveyor belt. The base was brown with steps going up one side and the large crane in the middle, which could be moved around. Like the UK version, the factory came with interchangeable plastic parts that could be used to make five different robots. These small parts are easily lost, so finding a mint set with all the pieces can be quite tough. Also, it's worth noting that Kenner re-released the Droid Factory as The Jabba the Hutt Dungeon when Return of the Jedi hit cinemas in 1983. This version included typical action figures, rather than robots you could build

yourself.

Another one of the more unusual playsets was the Land of the Jawas, which sounds slightly more impressive than the reality of what the toy delivered. One of the early scenes in Star Wars features the dwarf-like hooded Jawas who travel around in their massive Sandcrawler vehicle selling and buying robots. Luke and Uncle Owen purchase R2-D2 and C-3PO from the Jawas and this scene could be recreated thanks to the playset. As for the playset, there's a card backdrop of the Sandcrawler, with working elevator to take the droids away, and a plastic base to represent the desert-like landscape of the planet Tatooine.

Although the American version was virtually identical, the Kenner take on the so-called Land of the Jawas included a much better

plastic base with caves for the Jawas to hide in and a neat replica of the crashed pod that C-3PO and R2-D2 used to escape from Princess Leia's spaceship after Darth Vader invaded. So good was the base that Kenner decided to reuse it for the later Hoth Ice Planet and Rebel Command Center sets.

Sadly that was it for the Palitoy playsets, as Kenner began to produce the majority of the Star Wars merchandise from Empire Strikes Back onwards, while Palitoy basically became just a marketing and sales department rather than a toy producer. However, that's not to say the later playsets were no good and Kenner did release some extremely eye-catching sets inspired by The Empire Strikes Back and Return of the Jedi. However, for us, the originals are still the best! ■

Corgi Toys No. 336 James Bond Toyota 2000 GT, mint, superb example. Inner pictorial stand is near mint in a mint box. Sold for £320, Vectis, September.

Corgi Toys No. GS22 James Bond Gift Set, including Lotus Esprit, Aston Martin DB5, Moonraker space shuttle and satellite. Overall condition appears to be generally mint. Sold for £240, Vectis, September.

Cecil Coleman James Bond 007 No. 111/10186 Action Figure, extremely rare issue dressed as Commander Bond. Overall condition appears to be generally mint in an excellent plus You Only Live Twice lift off lid box. Sold for £900, Vectis, September.

Belkin Tinplate Mechanical Joker Figure, mint in a near mint lift off lid box, comes complete with folded leaflet and correct key. Sold for £50, Vectis, September.

Lone Star James Bond Sniper Rifle, overall condition is generally near mint in an excellent colourful card box. Sold for £700, Vectis, September.

Tower Press Supercar Deep Sea Adventure jigsaw, complete with original box, made 1961. Sold for £38, Mullock's, October.

Herbert No. 742 Doctor Who, comes complete with hat and scarf, overall condition appears to be generally mint, still tied down to back card. Sold for £50, Vectis, September.

Lone Star James Bond 100 Shot Repeater Cap Pistol, condition is generally mint in an excellent colourful card box. Sold for £190, Vectis, September.

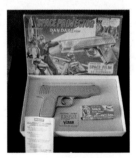

Merit Dan Dare Space Projector Gun, comes with film strip, overall condition is mint in excellent picture box. Sold for £200, Mullock's, October.

Eidai Grip Corporation James Bond Lotus Esprit from The Spy Who Loved Me, mint in a generally excellent plus box. Sold for £640, Vectis, September.

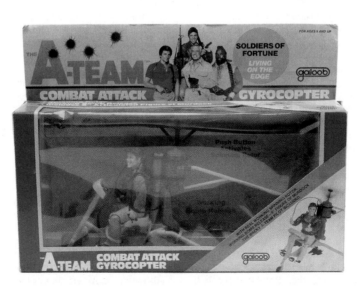

Galoob The A-Team No. 8516 Combat Attack Gyrocopter, complete with 'Mad Dog' Murdock figure. Mint in a good plus window box. Sold for £30, Vectis, September.

Shinsha Gerry Anderson's Thunderbird 5 No. 73105, colourful blue, yellow, red and dark blue model, mint, within good plus to excellent box. Sold for £80, Vectis, December.

Lincoln International Batman Escape Gun, dual action gun with darts and launcher wheels, housed on original illustrated card. Sold for £45, Mullock's, October.

Chad Valley Doctor Who Give-a-Show Projector, made 1965, battery-powered projector in original box with 16 slide-strips. Some slides are slightly bent. Sold for £95, Mullock's, October.

Lone Star No. 1208 James Bond Space Gun from the film Moonraker, mint including inner plastic tray, outer window box is excellent. Sold for £80, Vectis, September.

Lone Star Batman plastic cap gun, some distortion and losses to paint, slight cracking to one side of plastic. Sold for £150 Mullock's, October.

Corgi Toys No. 201 Volvo P1800 The Saint's Car, mint in orange and yellow window box. Sold for £220, Vectis, September.

Lone Star The Man from UNCLE 7.63mm automatic gun, gun has a cracked piece in the handle, comes complete with holster and belt - great example. Sold for £90, Mullock's, October.

Corgi Rockets No. 905 Volvo P1800 The Saint's Car, condition is generally mint, complete with key. Sold for £90, Vectis, September.

BBC TV Doctor Who and the Daleks jigsaw, made 1965, more than 185 pieces, in original box. Sold for £160, Mullock's, October.

Mettoy Dan Dare tinplate Ray Gun, 52cm long, in near mint condition, complete with sparking flint and illustrated box. Sold for £700, Mullock's, October.

Lone Star Stingray metal gun, over all condition is playworn, unboxed. Trigger hammer missing but still works. Sold for £30, Mullock's, October.

Marx Mary Poppins Whirling Toy, good plus example, made 1964. Sold for £95, Mullock's, October.

Lone Star No. 1269 James Bond Pistol, based on the one used in The Man with the Golden Gun, excellent plus in a good plus presentation box, some tears to cellophane. Sold for £140, Vectis, September.

Corgi Toys No. 268 The Green Hornet Black Beauty, complete with correct inner packing piece, sealed instruction pack, missiles and spinners. Sold for £300, Vectis, September.

Corgi Toys GS3 Batman Gift Set, including Batmobile with figures and Batboat on gold trailer, in mint condition. Sold for £380, Vectis, September.

Corgi Toys No. 1363 Buck Rogers Set, including Star Fighter in white and smaller Juniors issue, both are generally near mint in a good plus box. Sold for £50, Vectis, September.

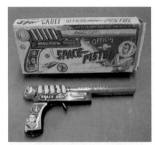

Marx Tom Corbett Space Cadet tinplate Space Pistol, excellent condition, 26cm long in original illustrated box (box missing one inner flap off each side). Sold for £160, Mullock's, October.

Biliken Mechanical Batman, near mint to mint, with excellent plus original box. Sold for £110, Mullock's, October.

Dinky Toys No. 102 Joe 90 Joe's Car, finished in aqua, chrome trim with a red plastic thruster. Mint including inner pictorial stand. Sold for £380, Vectis, September.

Dinky Toys No. 103 Captain Scarlet Spectrum Patrol Car, rare variation with grey plastic aerial. Mint including carded picture box. Sold for £340, Vectis, September.

Pedigree Products Captain Scarlet Action Figure, overall condition appears to be generally mint in an excellent box, circa 1967. Sold for £360, Vectis, September.

Dinky Toys No. 105 Captain Scarlet Maximum Security Vehicle, first issue finished in white, with red side stripes, orange interior and radiation box. Mint. Sold for £360, Vectis, September.

Merit Dan Dare Rocket Gun, rare issue finished in copper, complete with inner carded tray and great illustrated box. Sold for £140, Mullock's, October.

Kenner Star Wars Jawa with vinyl cape, figure is dusty with some paint wear to hands, cape has some grubby marks and dent on back. Sold for £380, Aston's, September.

Century 21 Toys Captain Scarlet Spectrum Patrol Car, large plastic issue has all its accessories, overall condition is generally excellent plus (although some small glue marks near rear fin). Reproduction inner packing piece. Sold for £100, Vectis, September.

Merit Dan Dare Planet Gun, near mint, complete with good illustrated box. Sold for £65, Mullock's, October.

Dinky Toys No. 351 Shado UFO Interceptor, mint including inner pictorial stand. Sold for £280, Vectis, September.

Mego Star Trek Ilia 3 3/4" action figure, sealed on good card, Blu-Tac to all four back corners. Sold for £25, Aston's, September.

Lincoln International Remote Controlled Stingray, condition is generally mint in a generally excellent colourful lift off lid box. Reproduction inner packing pieces. Sold for £480, Vectis, September.

Lone Star The Avengers Steed's Sword Stick, overall condition is generally near mint, including original card with accessories still attached. Sold for £500, Vectis, September.

Codeg Doctor Who Clockwork Dalek, finished in blue, silver and gold, made from tinplate and plastic, comes complete with key. Overall condition is generally near mint. Sold for £220, Vectis, September.

Lone Star Starsky & Hutch Cap Pistol, overall condition is generally near mint, although it does have a couple of small marks around cap loading area. In a generally good plus to excellent picture box. Sold for £60, Vectis, September.

Louis Marx Dalek Shooting Game, cardboard display is a little creased and worn especially to edges but is otherwise good, tin targets (one each in red and yellow, gold and blue, blue and yellow and green and yellow) are good plus to excellent, gun is good plus within excellent plus original box. Sold for £580, Vectis, December.

Product Enterprise Gerry Anderson Fireball XL5 World Space Patrol diecast model, excellent and boxed. Sold for £150, Aston's, September.

Merit (J&L Randall Ltd.) The Avengers Shooting Game, circa 1967, issue is generally near mint in an excellent colourful lift off lid box – does have a couple of small stains. Sold for £750, Vectis, September.

Mattel Mork and Mindy Robin Williams as Mork with Talking Spacepack, excellent in good box. Sold for £45, Aston's, September.

Mattel Battlestar Galactica Ovion action figure, sealed on very good unpunched card. Sold for £25, Aston's, October.

Ben Cooper Star Wars The Empire Strikes Back Yoda Costume and Mask, large, excellent in good box. Sold for £20, Aston's, October.

Airfix James Bond Special Agent 007 Aston Martin DB5 1/24 scale plastic model kit, appears complete with instructions in good plus box. Sold for £150, Aston's, October.

Kenner No. 46000 Indiana Jones 12-inch Action Figure from Raiders of the Lost Ark, circa 1981 issue, overall condition is generally mint in a near mint presentation window box. Sold for £110, Vectis, September.

Kenner No. 70060 Alien Figure, made 1979, issue is generally mint complete with instruction sheet, outer window box is good plus. Sold for £100, Vectis, September.

Mego/Burbank Toys Wonder Woman, 12" tall fully poseable doll, copyright 1976, complete with stand, figure is excellent plus to near mint condition within good plus window box. Sold for £120, Vectis, December.

Mego Flash Gordon Playset, 1978, one side is Ming's Throne Room complete with throne the other side is Dr. Zarkov's Secret Laboratory with a simulated computer, this computer only contains one computer card - Dale Arden, set is in good condition. Sold for £15, Vectis, December.

Ljn V Enemy Visitor Action figure, 1984 issue, mint, sealed within excellent plus (cellophane yellowed) box. Sold for £60, Vectis, December.

Fairylite Fireball XL5 Steve Zodiac Space Gun, a plastic water pistol. very good condition. Sold for £35, Aston's, October.

Aurora 412-129 The Man From UNCLE Illya Kuryakin with Dimensional Background, appears complete (not checked), with instructions in good but scuffed box. Sold for £50, Aston's, October.

Corgi Juniors Superman Set, comprising of Daily Planet Helicopter; Daily Planet Delivery Van, Supermobile and City of Metropolis Police Car. Conditions are generally mint on near mint to mint blister cards, carded sleeve is excellent plus. Sold for £80, Vectis, December.

Corgi Juniors Super Heroes Gift Set No.56105, comprising of Spider-Man - Spidercopter; Batman - Batcopter; Superman - Daily Planet Helicopter and Daily Planet Delivery Van. Conditions appear to be generally mint on near mint to mint blister cards. Carded sleeve is excellent. Sold for £70, Vectis, December.

Codeg Dr. Who Dodge The Daleks game, 1964, dice shaker and four plastic playing pieces complete with plastic dice, colourfully illustrated game board, condition is excellent within excellent beautifully illustrated box. Sold for £280, Vectis, December.

Kenner The Real Ghostbusters ECTO 1, carefully opened to one end is mint, transfers unapplied, within good plus to excellent box. Sold for £130, Vectis, December.

Azrak-Hamway International Inc plastic Batmobile, copyright 1976, Hong Kong plastic, good plus complete with Batman and Robin figures. Sold for £25, Vectis, December.

Marx Toys Dr. Who Robot Action battery operated Dalek, copyright BBC 1974, scarce yellow issue, complete with eye, sucker and gun. Near mint within good plus to excellent box complete with inner packaging band. Sold for £60, Vectis, December.

Avon Batmobile blue plastic bubble bath, copyright 1978, excellent plus within good plus to excellent box. Sold for £30, Vectis, December.

Bell Toys Doctor Who's 'Astro Ray' Dalek Gun, early 1965 issue, complete with three Ray Beam Ray Darts, uses type U11 batteries, untested. Excellent to excellent plus, within excellent (small tear to surface paper to one corner and slight scuffing to edges box), marked in pencil 14/11 to top lid. Sold for £500, Vectis, December.

Merit Dan Dare Walkie-Talkie Set, finished in red/black, blue/yellow and green plastic. Excellent plus to near mint within good plus to excellent brightly illustrated box. Sold for £25, Vectis, December.

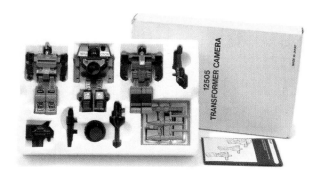

Hasbro Transformers G1 Reflector Mailaway, including Spectro Robot, Viewfinder Robot and Spyglass Robot, Shutter Gun, Lens Laser, Optoblaster, Telephoto three missiles, transfers are applied, items are near mint, complete with instruction leaflet and box. Sold for £110, Vectis, December.

Powertronic by Nasta Transformers Robot AM Radio, copyright 1984, finished in red and blue plastic with silver detail, comes with a "mock-up" box. Sold for £70, Vectis, December.

Hasbro Transformers G1 Series 4 Fortress Maximus, copyright 1987, mint, still sealed within excellent box. Sold for £1,300, Vectis, December.

Pedigree Gerry Anderson's Captain Scarlet Destiny Angel, excellent, boxed, sealed in original cellophane. Sold for £40, Aston's, October.

Marx Toys Lone Ranger in the Adventure of the Lost Cavalry Patrol Outfit No. 7430, excellent, unopened, boxed. Sold for £30, Aston's, October.

Kenner The Real Ghostbusters Peter Venkman and Grabber Ghost, figure is near mint apart from slight degradation to plastic on left leg, within good plus to excellent bubble, has indentations in places, on good plus card. Sold for £70, Vectis, December.

Lone Star The Man From UNCLE 7.63mm cap-firing pistol, good, some corrosion and paint wear, on fair backing card, some creases, edges scuffed, tear around cut out badge. Sold for £55, Aston's, October.

Vivid Imaginations Captain Scarlet Spectrum Camp Base HQ, item is mint, factory sealed within excellent plus box. Sold for £20, Vectis, December.

Mattel Masters of The Universe Two Bad No. 9040, mint within excellent plus bubble, upon excellent plus card. Sold for £50, Vectis, December.

Mattel Masters of The Universe Roboto No. 9041, mint, within excellent plus bubble upon excellent card. Sold for £45, Vectis, December.

Mattel Masters of The Universe Moss Man No. 9219, mint, within excellent plus bubble upon excellent card. Sold for £50, Vectis, December.

Mattel Masters of The Universe Tung Lashor No. 2331, mint, within good plus (slightly crushed) bubble and excellent plus to near mint card. Sold for £40, Vectis, December.

Corgi Toys The Green Hornet's Black Beauty No. 268, nearly mint in nearly excellent box with excellent inner pictorial stand, transparent decal sheet cover, packing piece, Secret Instruction packet containing Secret Instructions, three spinners and three rockets. Sold for £110, Warwick & Warwick, November.

JR21 Thunderbirds Lady Penelope's FAB 1, plastic friction drive with Parker and Lady Penelope figures, machine guns at front, nearly mint in nearly excellent box with packing piece. Sold for £48, Warwick & Warwick, November.

Kenner The Real Ghostbusters Ray Stantz and Wrapper Ghost, near mint to mint, within good plus to excellent bubble (has some indentation), upon mainly excellent un-punched card. Sold for £70, Vectis, December.

Denys Fisher The Bionic Woman 12″ poseable Jamie Sommers figure, plastic to bionic arm has degraded slightly otherwise excellent plus, still retained within original packaging, complete with factory sealed baggie containing accessories, instruction leaflet and mission purse within good original box. Sold for £80, Vectis, December.

Mattel Masters of The Universe Hordak No. 9172, mint, within good (yellowed and slightly crushed) bubble upon good plus card. Sold for £45, Vectis, December.

Mattel Masters of The Universe Modulok No. 9174, mint, sealed within excellent plus box. Sold for £60, Vectis, December.

Gilbert James Bond tinplate battery operated Aston Martin DB5 Goldfinger and Thunderball, silver, chrome trim, comes complete with bandit figure. - overall condition is Near Mint, a superb example - in generally good to good plus lift-off lid colour picture box, inner polystyrene packaging is good. Sold for £340, Vectis, December.

Crescent Matt Helm Secret Agent ICE 100 Shot Repeater and Holster, sub-sonic silencer and infra-red telescopic sight, very good on good backing card. Sold for £130, Aston's, October.

Knickerbocker Star Trek Soft Poseable Mr. Spock, 1979, in original packaging. Sold for £18, East Bristol Auctions, January.

Popy (Japan) Gerry Anderson's Space: 1999 Eagle vehicle, vehicle still within polystyrene packaging, missiles still factory sealed within original plastic bag, complete with instruction leaflet, rare model. Sold for £180, Vectis, December.

Codeg Dr. Who mechanical Dalek, tinplate and plastic, copyright, 1965, finished in blue, silver and gold, complete with eye, sucker and gun, original key. Excellent plus to near mint within excellent Plus original box. Sold for £300, Vectis, December.

Kenner MASK Detonator, 1980s, appears complete with original box, including some interior packaging. Three figures. Sold for £34, East Bristol Auctions, January.

Mattel Inc. Toy Makers Chitty Chitty Bang Bang, this plastic issue comes complete with raft and figures, overall condition appears to be near mint in generally excellent plus (opened) carded picture box. Sold for £100, Vectis, December.

Corgi Toys The Saint's Volvo P1800 No. 258, white body, red label, red interior, good plus in good box. Sold for £60, Warwick & Warwick, November.

Kenner MASK Meteor, 1980s, boxed, with action figure. Sold for £32, East Bristol Auctions, January.

Codeg Dr. Who mechanical Dalek, tinplate and plastic, copyright 1965, finished in silver, black and gold, complete with eye, sucker and gun arm, complete with original key. Near mint, excellent plus box, has pencil notation 15/11R to lid. The box has also got original packaging. Sold for £400, Vectis, December.

Palitoy Doctor Who Talking K-9, 1978, in original box with disc and original inner packaging. Sold for £160, East Bristol Auctions, January.

Kenner The Real Ghostbusters Fright Features Ray Stantz, 1980s, card unpunched and unopened. Sold for £18, East Bristol Auctions, March.

Kenner The Real Ghostbusters Highway Haunter Action Ghost Vehicle, VW Beetle convertible, mint, factory sealed within near mint box. Sold for £50, Vectis, December.

Glasslite Star Wars Power of the Force X-Wing (Brazil), 'Caca Estelar ASA-X Motorizado', good plus, complete with good plus box. Sold for £420, Vectis, April.

Mattel Planet of the Apes No. 730 Tommy-Burst Gun with Ape Mask, circa 1967, overall generally near mint, mask good plus to excellent, back card is good plus. Won from a Daily Mirror competition, complete with original congratulations letter. Sold for £540, Vectis, February.

Corgi Toys No. 268 The Green Hornet Black Beauty, complete with spinning disc to rear and missile to front, unboxed. Sold for £38, East Bristol Auctions, January.

Corgi Toys No. 271 James Bond 007 Aston Martin DB5, complete in original box. Sold for £80, East Bristol Auctions, January.

Kenner MASK Stinger, 1980s, in original box. Sold for £34, East Bristol Auctions, January.

Mattel Masters of the Universe He-Man Pinball, 1983, in original box. Sold for £32, East Bristol Auctions, March.

Kenner The Real Ghostbusters Ecto 3, appearing unused in all original packaging - believed to be untouched since purchase. Sold for £36, East Bristol Auctions, March.

Corgi Toys No. 266 Chitty Chitty Bang Bang, complete with all original figures and wings, unboxed. Sold for £40, East Bristol Auctions, January.

Kenner Star Wars Return of the Jedi plus Paploo the Ewok, complete with swing label, excellent plus to near mint. Sold for £40, Vectis, April.

Merit Dan Dare Space Control Radio Station, complete with original box, set appears unused. With instructions and internal packaging. Sold for £90, East Bristol Auctions, March.

Kenner Star Wars Return of the Jedi plush Wicket W. Warrick the Ewok, complete with swing label, excellent plus to near mint in good plus box. Sold for £40, Vectis, April.

Dinky Toys No. 101 Thunderbird 2, complete with Thunderbird 4 pod, overall condition is generally excellent, inner pictorial stand is good plus to excellent, outer box is good plus. Sold for £320, Vectis, February.

Merit Dan Dare Rocket Gun, complete with two plastic darts, in original illustrated box. Sold for £150, Biddle & Webb, March.

Palitoy/ General Mills Star Wars Return of the Jedi Tri-log plush Mookie the Ewok, excellent plus to near mint in excellent plus to near mint box. Sold for £50, Vectis, April.

Kenner Star Wars Return of the Jedi Laser Rifle Carry Case, excellent plus to near mint, with excellent packaging. Sold for £120, Vectis, April.

Don Post Studios Star Wars Yoda Latex Mask, excellent plus, within good plus to excellent correct box. Sold for £50, Vectis, April.

Dinky Toys No. 103 Captain Scarlet Spectrum Patrol Car, excellent plus, nice bright example in a generally good plus box. Sold for £110, Vectis, February.

Kenner Star Wars The Empire Strikes Back Star Destroyer, diecast and plastic spaceship, mint within near mint bubble, excellent box. Sold for £110, Vectis, April.

Corgi Toys No. 807 The Magic Roundabout Dougal's Car, extra decals applied, excellent condition though does require cleaning, in a generally good plus to excellent box. Sold for £70, Vectis, February.

Kenner Star Wars Micro Collection Bespin Freeze Chamber Action Playset, excellent, contents unchecked for completeness, excellent plus box. Sold for £90, Vectis, April.

Corgi Toys No. 267 Batman Batmobile, generally excellent plus, in a generally good plus inner pictorial stand with instruction pack containing leaflet and some missiles, outer box is good to good plus. Sold for £260, Vectis, February.

Don Post Studios Star Wars Darth Vader Mask, good plus within fair to good box. Sold for £70, Vectis, April.

Gilbert James Bond Battery Operated Aston Martin DB5, from Goldfinger and Thunderball, with bandit figure and swing tag attached to car, in original box. Sold for £550, Biddle & Webb, March.

Cox Star Wars Luke Skywalker's Landspeeder, glow fuel powered remote control, mint, in excellent plus box. Sold for £40, Vectis, April.

Ideal Evel Knievel Stunt Cycle, in original box with two figures. Sold for £70, East Bristol Auctions, January.

Corgi Comics No. 801 Noddy, Big Ears and Golly Car, in original window box. Sold for £200, Biddle & Webb, March.

Corgi Toys No. 320 The Saint Jaguar XJS, in original box with unfolded header card, model is rubbed to one side from rubbing the box insert. Sold for £40, Lacy, Scott & Knight, February.

Mattel Masters of the Universe He-Man Castle Grayskull, in original box, complete including interior pieces and instructions. Sold for £95, East Bristol Auctions, January.

Hasbro Transformers G1 Galvatron, in original box. Sold for £32, East Bristol Auctions, January.

Mettoy Batman Spin Dart Target Game, including colourful tinplate card target, Bat gun and two darts. Condition is excellent plus in a hard to find full colour picture box. Sold for £750, Vectis, February.

Ideal The Dukes of Hazzard Electronic Slot Racing Set, including General Lee and Police car, overall condition appears to be generally excellent plus to mint. Sold for £45, Vectis, February.

Corgi Toys No. 930 James Bond 007 Moonraker Drax Jet Ranger, in original box, appears unused, with original band still holding helicopter in box. Sold for £50, East Bristol Auctions, January.

Kenner Star Wars Luke Skywalker AM Headset Radio, mint (still within factory plastic), with inner polystyrene packaging, instruction leaflet, excellent box. Sold for £200, Vectis, April.

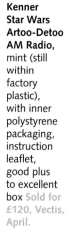

Kenner Star Wars Artoo-Detoo AM Radio, mint (still within factory plastic), with inner polystyrene packaging, instruction leaflet, good plus to excellent box Sold for £120, Vectis, April.

Ideal The Professionals Electronic Slot Road Racing Set, including Ford Capri and 'Security' Van plus track and accessories. Generally near mint to mint. Sold for £130, Vectis, February.

Arcofaic Star Wars Baby Flippers Pinball Game, good but missing balls. Sold for £100, Vectis, April.

Lone Star Dan Dare Space Gun, made in 1950s, red colouring. Complete with reproduction box. Sold for £30, East Bristol Auctions, January.

Kenner Star Wars Micro Collection Death Star Escape Playset, mint, sealed in excellent plus to near mint box. Sold for £70, Vectis, April.

Kenner Star Wars Micro Collection Bespin Gantry Action Playset, mint, sealed in near mint box Sold for £70, Vectis, April.

Kenner Star Wars Micro Collection Hoth Turret Defense Playset, mint, sealed in near mint box. Sold for £70, Vectis, April.

Takara Star Wars C-3PO, missile firing diecast and plastic figure, No. 410201-0, near mint with one missile, in good plus box with inner packaging. Sold for £90, Vectis, April.

Kenner Star Wars Micro Collection Hoth Wampa Cave Playset, mint, sealed in near mint box. Sold for £70, Vectis, April.

Takara Star Wars Darth Vader, missile firing diecast and plastic figure, No. 410202-2, mint, with sealed bag containing weapon/accessories, in excellent plus box with packaging. Sold for £200, Vectis, April.

Takara/General Mills Star Wars R2-D2, missile firing diecast figure, mint in excellent box. Sold for £100, Vectis, April.

Kenner Star Wars Micro Collection Hoth Generator Attack Playset, mint, sealed in near mint box. Sold for £70, Vectis, April.

Kenner Star Wars Preschool Wicket the Ewok Discovery Time Sit 'n' Spin Ride On Toy, near mint in excellent box. Sold for £50, Vectis, April.

Palitoy Star Wars Luke Skywalker's Three Position Laser Rifle, near mint to mint in excellent box. Sold for £240, Vectis, April.

Kenner Star Wars Micro Collection Bespin Control Room Action Playset, mint, sealed in near mint box. Sold for £70, Vectis, April.

Meccano Star Wars Robot R2-D2 Radio Commande, near mint to mint, with instructions in excellent box. Sold for £90, Vectis, April.

Takara Star Wars R2-D2, missile firing diecast and plastic figure, No. 410024-4, mint, transfers unapplied, with instructions, missiles still on sprue, in good plus box with inner packaging. Sold for £160, Vectis, April.

Kenner Star Wars Battery Operated Toothbrush, mint, sealed within excellent plus bubble, excellent un-punched card. Sold for £130, Vectis, April.

Corgi Toys No. 497 The Man from UNCLE, near mint, beautiful example, inner pictorial stand is excellent plus, with inner packing piece but missing Waverly Ring, outer box is good plus to excellent. Sold for £160, Vectis, February.

Kenner Star Wars Return of the Jedi See-Threepio Collectors Case, near mint, in good packaging. Sold for £70, Vectis, April.

Dinky Toys No. 104 Captain Scarlet Spectrum Pursuit Vehicle, overall condition is generally good plus to excellent, in a good plus inner pictorial stand with correct instruction sheet, outer box is good with some small tears. Sold for £120, Vectis, February.

Matchbox Gerry Anderson's Thunderbirds Tracy Island Electronic Playset, mint, sealed, together with outer carton. Sold for £70, Vectis, August.

Denys Fisher Dr Who Leela poseable figure, overall condition is generally near mint on a good plus backing card, outer box is good. Sold for £220, Vectis, February.

Mettoy Dan Dare 'Eagle'Spaceship, tinplate, with fly wheel motor mechanism, complete with original illustrated box. Sold for £300, Biddle & Webb, March.

Dinky Toys No. 358 Star Trek USS Enterprise, complete with pod, overall condition is generally excellent plus (does have some very slight discolouration marks), in a generally good plus to excellent carded picture box. Sold for £70, Vectis, August.

Stoddard lead hollowcast Mikey Mouse, wearing green shorts and yellow shoes, on an oval base. Height approximately 5.5cm. Sold for £140, Toovey's, March.

Hasbro Transformers G1 Jetfire, with original box. Sold for £55, East Bristol Auctions, January.

Corgi Toys No. 808 Basil Brush and his Car, within the original box. Sold for £60, East Bristol Auctions, March.

Kenner The Real Ghostbusters Ghostzapper, within original box and with cardboard inner. Sold for £38, East Bristol Auctions, March.

Dapol Doctor Who Ice Warrior WO13, unopened. Sold for £16, East Bristol Auctions, March.

Palitoy BBC Talking Dalek, appears complete with eyepiece, gun and 'plunger' within the original box. Sold for £70, East Bristol Auctions, July.

Reel Spider-Man Remote Control Car, with original box. Sold for £28, East Bristol Auctions, July.

DIECAST | RAILWAYS | TOY FIGURES | TINPLATE | TV & FILM | OTHERS | EBUYS

Corgi Toys No. 261 James Bond's Aston Martin DB5, all complete with the original Secret Documents, two ejector seat figures, Collectors Club slip and display stand. Sold for £150, East Bristol Auctions, July.

Palitoy Vinyl Cape Jawa vintage 3 3/4" figure, with weapon, good plus to excellent. Sold for £700, Vectis, June.

Palitoy Bonanza Little Joe 'The Moveable Man', with authentic accessories, 1966 issue, 8" figure with gun, holster, hat, belt, spurs, water bottle and lasso. Near mint, good plus box. Sold for £80, Vectis, June.

Kenner The Real Ghostbusters Fire Station Headquarter complete within the original box, including traps, railings and fire pole. Sold for £65, East Bristol Auctions, July.

Denys Fisher The Bionic Woman, appears complete with original box, including inner cardboard sleeve, 'mission purse' and instructions. Figure still attached to card. Sold for £100, East Bristol Auctions, July.

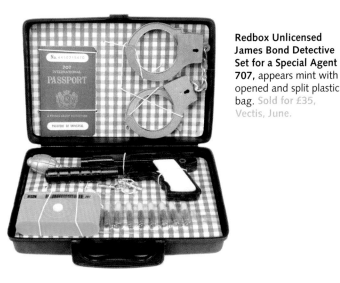

Redbox Unlicensed James Bond Detective Set for a Special Agent 707, appears mint with opened and split plastic bag. Sold for £35, Vectis, June.

Popy Bandai Battle of the Planets Gatch-Spaltan Spacecraft, near mint to mint in a good plus sealed box. Sold for £70, Vectis, June.

Popy Bandai Battle of the Planets God Phenix Spacecraft, near mint to mint in a good plus sealed box. Sold for £100, Vectis, June.

Corgi The Saint's Jaguar XJS, within the original box, 'Sonic Control' plastic gun included, with interior packaging. Sold for £24, East Bristol Auctions, July.

Playmates Teenage Mutant Ninja Turtles Knucklehead Attack 'n Grab Foot Machine, boxed. Sold for £20, Vectis, August.

Palitoy Bradgate Marvel Comics Superheroes Game, appears complete and virtually unused. Sold for £36, East Bristol Auctions, July.

Sears Tara Toys Marvel Hulk Hide-away Playcase, mint, still factory sealed within original excellent box. Sold for £90, Vectis, August.

Kenner The Real Ghostbusters ECTO-1A Action Vehicle, 100% complete with original box and unused decals. Sold for £55, East Bristol Auctions, July.

Introduction to... Other Toys & games

In this section you'll find a wide variety of vintage toys, from well known names like Airfix or Meccano to little known manufacturers from around the world.

The 'other' category is the slightly unglamorous name for the various toys, games and collectables that appear at toy auctions throughout the year but wouldn't really fill their own category. Here you'll find the likes of Scalextric, Meccano, LEGO, Action Man, plastic kits and plenty more. Although they're all put together, that doesn't mean they're not as important as the categories featured previously and, as you'll see, some of the toys (particularly the Meccano) achieve fantastic prices at auction houses.

As you can tell from that introduction though, the 'others' section still contains plenty of household names, like Meccano, Airfix and Scalextric. Interestingly, all three have their links with Hornby too – Meccano was invented by Frank Hornby, while Airfix and Scalextric are now both run under the Hornby Hobbies umbrella, which also includes Corgi.

In terms of value, it's those early Meccano sets and some of the Constructor series (including planes and cars) that tend to fetch the big money in the saleroom. Some of those original

sets also came in superb wooden cases, complete with drawers and various compartments, so it's easy to see why these have become such attractive pieces.

Another popular choice is, of course, Scalextric. Originally launched in 1957 by Fred Francis, the original Scalextric slot cars were actually made in tinplate, rather than plastic, and have become very sought after today. Rather than the larger sets, it's often the individual cars that are worth the most when it comes to Scalextric, particularly the early plastic ones after Fred Francis sold Scalextric to Lines Bros.

One of the other household names you'll see crop up in the pages ahead is Action Man. Although released by British firm Palitoy on these shores, Action Man was based on the American GI Joe character developed by Hasbro. Seen by many as the original 'action figure' before Kenner came along with its 3 3/4-inch *Star Wars* figures, Palitoy was quick to expand on the GI Joe brand with new features (like flocked hair and those infamous 'eagle eyes'), outfits and vehicles. Interestingly some of the rare outfits can be worth a lot and earlier this year Vectis sold an

Action Man Judo Outfit for £5,400.

Along with TV and film toys, the 'other' category is another section where we're seeing plenty of items that many consider to be 'collectables of the future' that could potentially increase in price in the years to come. One of the most interesting is the fact that prices for old videogames and consoles (in their original boxes, of course) are starting to creep up and we're seeing more of these lots appear at auctioneers. In fact, Aston's had an entire section of a sale dedicated to empty boxes for SEGA Nintendo games earlier this year. ▪

121
You'll find 121 collectables listed in this category, covering a wide range of toys.

66
Action Man, who features heavily across the following pages, was launched in the UK in 1966.

£116
The average price paid this year in this section was £116.

£600
There were a number of items that sold for £600 - the highest price paid.

14,094
The grand total for the 'other' section is a mighty £14,742.

Game on?

Sheffield Auction Gallery's Phil Hughes talkes to us about a potential collectable of the future.

A collection of Nintendo Game & Watches, owned by Sheffield Auction Gallery's Phil Hughes.

Back in the 1950s or '60s, it's unlikely most children looked at the Corgi and Dinky diecast cars they were bashing into each other and thought "I better be more careful with these because I bet they'll be worth a fortune in the future". Likewise in the '70s as kids were recreating their favourite scenes from Star Wars (in one memorable case for me this involved pretending Luke Skywalker had been melted with a laser… otherwise known as setting fire to him with a lighter) they weren't concerned with keeping the box in mint condition, just in case they had a rare limited edition colour variation of Boba Fett. Hindsight is obviously a wonderful thing but wouldn't it be great to predict the collectables of the future? Well, one auctioneer thinks he may have spotted a new trend: videogames.

Phil Hughes, specialist valuer at Sheffield Auction Gallery, is an avid collector of all things electronic, as well as more unusual pieces like stuffed animals… something we're not going to look at here. While he's been collecting more and more electronica, Phil has noticed a growing trend in the popularity of older videogames from the 1970s and '80s. This, coupled with the fact that Sheffield Auction Gallery is seeing an increase in the amount of videogames being sold in its toy sales, has resulted in Phil predicting that videogames could be the next big thing in the world of collecting.

"So, we're talking about what we would call relatively modern hand-held computer games," explains Phil, "these are something that's coming into the auction a lot more at the moment and we're beginning to see an increased interest in this type of thing as opposed to the old, more established toys like Corgi, Dinky and Sutcliffe Submarines. It's definitely a younger generation of people that are remembering the toys of their youth and now they have a bit of disposable income, they're starting to collect them and some of them are becoming increasingly expensive and hard to find."

It's likely that many of us haven't even considered that these little bleeping electronic devices or dusty videogame consoles with their block graphics and simple controllers could be worth anything. They're probably sitting in the loft and feeling unloved but Phil suggests that now's the time to start digging them out and selling, as some are potentially worth a lot of money.

"The Nintendo Game & Watches are probably the most advanced in terms of collecting at the moment," Phil told us, "but there are other brands like Tomy, which produced quite a lot of different things. It did a 3D binocular type videogame and those are quite popular. Grandstand is a manufacturer that was around for just a few years but it made an awful lot of quite cheap, simple, one player, LCD games. So you'll see things like Tarzan and Munch Man from Grandstand a lot because they were among the most popular ones. But as you're looking around, if you see one that's a bit different, go for that because that's obviously going to be a rarer one and some them are really relatively quite expensive."

As Phil says, Nintendo Game & Watches are arguably the most popular vintage videogames, with some websites dedicated to listing price guides for these electronic games. They were first released in 1980 after Japanese game designer Gunpei Yoko saw a businessman 'playing' on a calculator by pressing the buttons. He then had the idea of creating a watch that could also double as a game machine to pass the time. The first Game & Watch was called Ball and featured a juggler who had to be moved

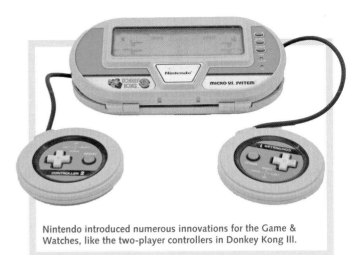

Nintendo introduced numerous innovations for the Game & Watches, like the two-player controllers in Donkey Kong III.

ABOVE
As well as old videogames, Phil is predicting that even old technology like calculators could become collectable in years to come.

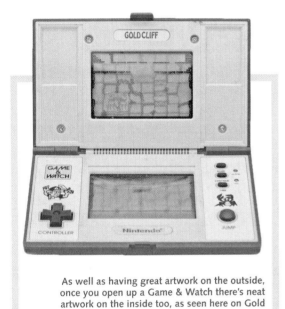

As well as having great artwork on the outside, once you open up a Game & Watch there's neat artwork on the inside too, as seen here on Gold Cliff, released in 1988.

ABOVE
Grandstand videogames were aimed at the budget market and were never as popular as Nintendo's offerings.

BELOW
This game only features a series of red LEDs that are meant to represent footballers... Grimsby Town uses it to create their match tactics.

ABOVE
Munchman is a blatant rip-off of the exceptionally popular Pac-Man series.

around the screen to catch three balls.

Originally the Game & Watch consoles were calculator-sized machines with just one screen and a few buttons but in 1982 Nintendo released a clamshell-style Game & Watch that featured two screens and could be closed to protect the screen from scratches... after all, these were meant to be kept in pockets, bags and even briefcases. In the same year, another big move came with the introduction of a cross-shaped button that could be used to move the character around the game screen... a design that would become commonplace in almost all future games consoles. Nintendo's final Game & Watch was Mario the Juggler, released in 1991. Fittingly it featured similar gameplay to the original Ball but starred Nintendo's new mascot, Mario.

But if you're hoping to start collecting these vintage videogames, what else should you be looking for? "There's a very established market on the internet for these things now and people are certainly looking for good quality examples that aren't broken," explained Phil. "Game & Watches had these clips on them which were susceptible to breaking so watch out for those, plus people are also very fussy about the serial numbers on the back and obviously it's better if you can get them boxed with the polystyrene, the instructions and the warranty card. People are getting increasingly more and more fussy rather than just filling their shelves up with old tech."

However, perhaps that most exciting thing is that because videogames are a growing market, some people aren't aware of their potential value, giving keen eyed dealers the opportunity to make a profit... but times are changing. "You can still pick this sort of thing up at boot fairs and you even get them occasionally in your charity shops," said Phil. "But people are cottoning on to this and you're not getting as lucky as you used to five or 10 years ago when there would just be a box full of them and you'd get them for a fiver because the little old lady didn't really know what she was selling.

"You certainly will find them at boot fairs and places like this. However, here in Sheffield, where we have a lot of younger people who are opening up antiques shops in the antiques quarter, some are concentrating more on this type of stuff rather than the traditional china and

that sort of thing. That is because it's what reminds them of their childhood, like Dinky Toys or Corgi remind an older generation of their childhood."

Don't worry if you're a diecast fan or collect model railways because Phil isn't predicting that videogames will be replacing them anytime soon. "I don't think they'll supersede the old toys because I think that there's going to be a market for those, and obviously there's a well established pricing structure for that sort of thing. I think it will be a slow process and, although we are getting increasing amounts of it at the auction house, it's still tending to be bundled into three or four per lot; whereas with the Dinkys and the Corgis, they're well established and it's more common to sell them in individual lots."

Victory Models Hillman Minx, 1/24 scale model in plastic, overall condition is very good, complete with original box. In working order. Sold for £95, Mullock's, October.

Merit Toys Merry Milkman, 1960s, in original box. Sold for £22, Mullock's, October.

Yonesowa Teddy the Artist Electro Toy, box does have some creasing and some staining. Toy is bright and clean but has been used. Sold for $300, Morphy Auctions, September.

Marx Bazooka Bagatelle, circa 1930s, in box. World War II-themed. Sold for $60, Morphy Auctions, September.

Betal Games Bus Conductor Outfit, complete with cap, ticket machine, tickets, badge, fare card and pencil. Very clean, appears unused. Sold for £35, Mullock's, October.

Tri-ang Minic Motorway M1504 The London Set, containing grey Rolls Royce, maroon Mercedes, oval of track and two controllers. Near mint. Sold for £70, Mullock's, October.

Rotor the Walking Giant Robot, Cragstan (Hong Kong), circa 1970. On/off switch is loose, spinning eyes do no work. Among the scarcest early plastic robots. Sold for $210, Morphy Auctions, September.

Telephone Bear with lights, original box marked Linemar, with some creasing and fading to lid. Sold for $210, Morphy Auctions, September.

Siren Stan the Spaceman's Gun , circa 1960s, gun has some chips and minor cracks on tip. Box has one corner split. Sold for $84, Morphy Auctions, September.

Coleco US Astronaut Space Helmet, circa 1950s, helmet shows light use but no cracks or breaks. Face shield has small cracks around mouth that are taped. Sold for $180, Morphy Auctions, September.

Cragstan (Japan) battery operated Jolly Peanut Vendor, 9"/23cm long - good plus to excellent scarce example in a good illustrated box. Sold for £80, Vectis Auctions, October.

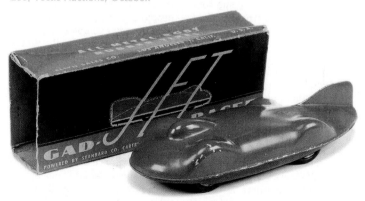

Penco Products (USA) aluminium Gad Jet Racer, good plus, comes in a fair card sleeve which lacks some of the end flaps. Sold for £110, Vectis Auctions, October.

Linemar (Japan) Sleeping Baby Bear, excellent condition with very little wear. The box has some minor tearing and creasing - the box bottom is not original. Sold for $420, Morphy Auctions, September.

Whittle Craft Stirling Moss Rally board game, in original box, with all components. Sold for £35, Mullock's, October.

Schuco Bigo-Bello Apache soft toy figure, lacks his axe head otherwise Good in a fair (torn) box. Sold for £20, Vectis Auctions, October.

Marx Toys (UK) Jungle Shooting Range, in original illustrated box. Sold for £35, Mullock's, October.

Ideal Astronaut Space Helmet, includes original box with slight creasing and wear. Condition is generally very good. Sold for $72, Morphy Auctions, September.

Mettoy (UK) Computacar, with electronic Chevrolet Corvette Stingray, red, with bollards and computer cards. Good plus to excellent including illustrated card box. Sold for £25, Vectis, December.

Marx Big Dial Blast Off pinball, includes original box, some creasing and wear. Toy itself is in nice condition. Sold for $48, Morphy Auctions, September.

VIP the Busy Boss, includes very difficult to find original box, some minor edge wear and creasing to box. Toy appears unused. Sold for $360, Morphy Auctions, September.

KK Masutoku Toy Factory (Japan) Modern Toys celluloid and clockwork novelty toy of a comical gentleman, large oversized head with insect, interchanging inset facial features when wound, dressed wearing a white shirt with lime green bow tie, pink waistcoat and jacket with blue trousers, mounted on a rectangular wooden plinth, 23cm high, boxed - illustrated printed label to lid. Sold for £260, Bamfords, October.

Monster Robot, made by ALPS (Japan), condition is near mint to near mint plus. Sold for $108, Morphy Auctions, September.

Mr. Fox the Magician Blowing Magical Bubbles, made by Yonezawa (Japan) and distributed by Cragstan. Toy looks like unused store stock. Sold for $360, Morphy Auctions, September.

Chad Valley Rocket Barrage shooting game, one dart missing, all housed in an illustrated box (some wear to lid). Sold for £65, Mullock's, October.

Steiff (Germany) cockerel trademark 'Steiff' button with black and yellow tag, 26cm high. Sold for £20, Bamfords, October.

Palitoy Vintage Action Man Astronaut, brown painted hair, complete non-gripping hands, some stress cracks. Accessories include propellant gun without crossbar, suit without rips, plus others. Overall condition is excellent. Sold for £40, Vectis, November.

Picnic Bunny, original box, marked 'ALPS', rabbit is in beautiful condition. Sold for $150, Morphy Auctions, September.

IMAI Jaguar XK-E Grand Touring Sport Coupe 1/8 scale model kit, unmade, in great condition box. Sold for £140, Mullock's, October.

Scalextric Set 60, consisting of Aston Martin, red and Ferrari, blue, both excellent to good, some white residue on Ferrari, track, instructions and other items, plus A209 Grandstand. Sold for £130, Tennants, December.

Steiff (Germany) riding turtle Slo, raised upon a metal frame with four painted red metal wheels with white rubber 'Steiff 80' tyres, handle bar, 57cm long, 1960s. Sold for £35, Bamfords, October.

Marx 'Johnny Apollo' Space Expedition, unused, neat mint old store stock, sealed and never opened. Scarce piece to find. Sold for $720, Morphy Auctions, September.

Scalextric C32 race tuned Mercedes 250 SL, finished in brown with white roof, blue driver with red helmet, racing number six with chrome detailed hubs, in the original window box with instruction leaflet. Sold for £55, Lacy, Scott & Knight, November.

Cragstan (Japan) Hobo the Accordion Player with Musical Chimp, some age wear but generally good overall in a fair illustrated box, which also has "Alps" labels, 10"/26cm tall. Sold for £40, Vectis Auctions, October.

LEGO promotional shop display plastic figure, wearing a white construction helmet, red zip up jacket with 'Lego' identification pass and blue trousers, 50cm high, with original display stand. Sold for £190, Bamfords, October.

Victory Models (UK) 1/18 scale Standard 10 Saloon, scarce large scale battery operated plastic model, RAF grey with beige tinplate inner seating, aluminium bumpers and fittings, steerable front wheels. Excellent in good illustrated box. Sold for £110, Vectis, December.

Clifford Series (Hong Kong) Vauxhall Vega Major Touring Coach, 10"/26cm plastic friction drive model similar to the Dinky Toys version - lilac with green interior and side stripe - ex-shop stock example. Near mint in excellent card box. Sold for £40, Vectis, December.

Clifford Series (Hong Kong) Vauxhall Vega Major Touring Coach, 10"/26cm plastic friction drive model similar to the Dinky Toys version - yellow with green interior and pink stripes, ex-shop stock example. Near mint in excellent illustrated box. Sold for £30, Vectis, December.

Hong Kong plastic Moon Scout Space Vehicle, battery operated with plated finish, some age wear but overall good plus including illustrated box with inner packaging, 6"/15cm. Sold for £20, Vectis, December.

Scalecraft (UK) electric Lotus 25 snap together model, blue, with racing number one, circa 1960s. Near mint in a good plus illustrated box with instructions. Sold for £10, Vectis, December.

Denys Fisher Cyborg figure, 8" clear plastic, based on the Japanese Shonen Toys by Takara, complete with removable transparent head, factory sealed weapons pack. Near mint, still retained upon card inner within good plus box with product leaflet. Sold for £120, Vectis, December.

Airfix Spitfire 'BTK', an original 1955 Edition, this is kit that originally launched Airfix's 1/72 scale Aircraft Series. Moulded in pale blue plastic. Generally Mint overall, contained in a generally mint first type (1955/59) illustrated header carded bag. Mint overall. Sold for £400, Vectis, December.

Palitoy Vintage Action Man Action Pilot, black painted hair, complete non-gripping hands, some stress cracks. Clothing includes metal dog tag, orange suit, blue cap, black boots. Also included is a reproduction box. Overall condition is good plus. Sold for £40, Vectis, November.

Paya (Spain) Mercedes Benz 220S 4-door Saloon, blue plastic body with tinplate baseplate and interior, friction drive to rear wheels, crack above front wheel arch otherwise good plus, 9.5"/24cm long. Sold for £60, Vectis, December.

Ideal Toy Company Motorific Fury Racerific remote control slot car set, comprising a yellow Triumph sports car, track pieces, checkpoint track piece, Y switches, cornering strip and starter timer. Sold for £10, Lacy, Scott & Knight, November.

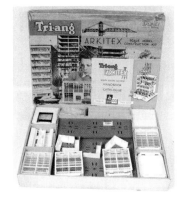

Tri-ang Spot-On Arkitex scale model construction set No. 1, contents are unchecked, with the original handbook/catalogue, heavily worn but all internal dividing sections are apparent, tape repair to box lid. Sold for £15, Lacy, Scott & Knight, November.

Scalextric C60, D-type Jaguar, yellow body with racing number 16, white driver with red hat, chrome exhaust, gold wash hubs, in the original Grand Prix flag box, some small tears to box insert. Sold for £45, Lacy, Scott & Knight, November.

Model Road Racing Cars Ltd (Bournemouth) Mercedes 154GP slot racing car, grey plastic body, No.2 with sticker sheet, excellent, box good. Sold for £70, Tennants, December.

Scalextric C/76 Mini Cooper, dark green body with brown interior, chrome hubs, in the original grand prix flag box with instructions. Sold for £25, Lacy, Scott & Knight, November.

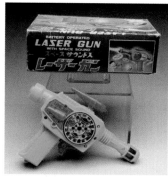

Japanese battery operated Laser Gun, Gun appears to be in unused and unplayed condition. Side of gun has a sticker that says "Laser Gun" on both sides. Also comes with original box; includes original insert. Sold for $210, Morphy Auctions, December.

Victory Industries (VIP Raceways) No.R63 BRM racing car, green body with racing number 5 labels with Club Special decal, chrome hubs with black tyres, in the original all card lift-off lid box with packing pieces. Very good condition. Sold for £50, Lacy, Scott & Knight, November.

Palitoy Vintage Action Man boxed Bullet Man, figure has been completely restrung to a high standard. Condition is good plus in a good plus box. Sold for £130, Vectis, November.

Meccano Aero Clockwork Motor No. 2, in the original blue all card box with key, instructions, various connecting rods and attachments and quality control label. Very good, box very good. Sold for £90, Lacy, Scott & Knight, November.

Palitoy Vintage Action Man boxed Captain Zargon Space Pirate, includes the usually missing visor and laser sword. Condition is excellent in good plus (tape to one end) box. Sold for £35, Vectis, November.

LEGO System No. 1242 Flag Set, five flags: Norway, Sweden, Denmark, Holland and a LEGO example, some losses and cleaning required, in the original sliding tray colourful box. Good condition. Sold for £20, Lacy, Scott & Knight, November.

Scalextric K-1 Go-Kart, light blue body with white driver, wearing a red helmet, black hubs, with silver detailed engine, in the original Grand Prix flag box. Sold for £50, Lacy, Scott & Knight, November.

Airfix 1/72 scale Aircraft Series 1, Type 2 Bagged Kits Second Issue (1959) R.E.8, generally mint overall, contained in a generally excellent (minor age wear) second type (1959/63) illustrated header carded bag. Sold for £60, Vectis, December.

F-500 Fury Space Gun, made from sturdy plastic, very few scratches, gun in great condition. With box and original instructions. Sold for $780, Morphy Auctions, December.

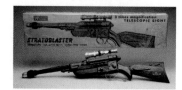

Plastic Stratoblaster, made of plastic, comes with original (repaired) box. Sold for $900, Morphy Auctions, December.

Denys Fisher Android figure, near mint to mint, with one green rocket (two are missing), still retained within original good box including inner packaging. Sold for £70, Vectis, December.

Playcraft N109 Home Farm Playset, of wooden, plastic and felt construction with four stables, fencing, grazing areas, clock and home farm sign, in the original buff and red coloured box. Sold for £10, Lacy, Scott & Knight, November.

Hubley The Red Fox Missile, plastic gun with missile attachment, gun appears to be in almost unused condition. Includes laser aim on top of gun. Includes box. Sold for $300, Morphy Auctions, December.

Maier Hancock Corporation Golf Master Set, practice device with golf ball on string, two tees, two fixing pins and instruction leaflet, in the original white and green black box, used otherwise good. Sold for £10, Lacy, Scott & Knight, November.

Rock'em Sock'em Robots, slight discoloration to one of the plastic robots. The toy is in working condition, the vinyl railings around the ring and decals are all marked "Rock'Em Sock'Em Robots by Marx". Sold for $180, Morphy Auctions, December.

Palitoy Vintage Action Man boxed Space Ranger Captain, suit is still supple. Condition is mainly good plus in good plus (tape marks) box. Sold for £30, Vectis, December.

Atomic Orbitor-X Space Game, two plastic guns, a little rockets attached and two canisters. Appears to be unplayed with and unopened. Sold for $180, Morphy Auctions, December.

Mettoy (UK) Standard Vanguard Fire Chief's Car, very scarce plastic bodied model to approximately 1/43 scale, tinplate base, friction drive. Good plus to excellent. Sold for £30, Vectis, December.

Lucky Toys (Hong Kong) friction drive Long Wheel Base Land Rover, red plastic model with fire chief livery. Near mint, approximately 1/32 scale. Sold for £40, Vectis, December.

Tri-ang Minic 1/20 scale Vauxhall Victor, scarce battery operated plastic model, green with tinplate tartan interior, lacks front and rear lamp, small crack and piece missing from rear off-side lamp assembly, chassis has been glued to body but still a fair to good example. Sold for £25, Vectis, December.

Marx Toys battery operated military SRN5 hovercraft, orange and green plastic body with yellow detailed fittings, battery operated flashing machine guns, appears complete with the original lift-off lid pictorial box, box is worn. Sold for £20, Lacy, Scott & Knight, November.

Ideal Tin Can Alley Game, 1970s children's shooting game, Pepsi can version, contents complete, in original box. Sold for £60, East Bristol Auctions, January.

LEGO No. 127 Train Set, 1970s, battery operated, boxed appearing complete with original instructions. Sold for £75, East Bristol Auctions, January.

Airfix 1/32 scale Bond Bug 700E Plastic Kit, appears complete with some wear, markings and creasings to the header, appears unopened. Sold for £110, Biddle & Webb, March.

Palitoy Action Man Scout Car, boxed with instructions. Sold for £36, East Bristol Auctions, January.

Airfix Motor Racing Slot Car Racing Set, containing E-Type Jaguar, Mini, Ford Zodiac, Ford Cortina and four open wheel racing cars, all good to fair. Sold for £130, Tennants, April.

Jetex Jet Propelled Racing Car, featuring black racing car with No. 11 driver, various accessories and fuel pellets, good to excellent for display, in a fair to good illustrated box. Sold for £35, Vectis, February.

Airfix 1/72 scale Aircraft Series 2 1962 De Havilland Mosquito VI, generally mint overall in a generally excellent first type (1962/63 only) illustrated set box. Sold for £280, Vectis, March.

Airfix 1/72 scale Aircraft Series 2 Second Issue 1963 Hawker Hunter F.6, generally mint overall in a generally excellent first type (1963 only) illustrated kit box. Sold for £350, Vectis, March.

Airfix 1/72 scale Aircraft Series 'Plasty' German 1957 De Havilland DH88, generally mint overall in a generally mint first issue German illustrated header carded bag. Sold for £30, Vectis, March.

Meccano Outfit No.10, with blue hatched/gold parts contained in original green three layer wooden box, with various instruction booklets. Parts fair, box has good original decals on outer and inner of lid, otherwise some retouching. Sold for £600, Tennants, December.

Lincoln International (Hong Kong) Large Electric 2.4 Jaguar, clean battery compartment, plated fittings, excellent plus. Sold for £50, Vectis, February.

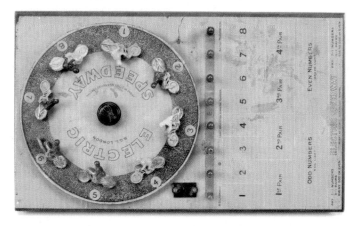

Electric Speedway Board Game, 1930s, made by BGL, contains a circular board with eight metal motorcycles with riders, illuminated bulbs and finishing posts. Sold for £60, Vectis, February.

Airfix 1/72 scale Aircraft Series 3 1960 Dornier 217E.2., generally mint overall in a generally near mint second type illustrated Series 3 set box. Sold for £130, Vectis, March.

Airfix 1/72 scale Aircraft Series First Issue Saunders Roe S-R.53, generally mint overall, in a generally excellent first type illustrated header carded bag. Sold for £60, Vectis, March.

Scalextric B/2 Hurricane Motorcycle and Sidecar, in the original Grand Prix flag all-card box, with packing piece and instruction leaflet, some cleaning required. Good condition, box good to very good. Sold for £65, Lacy, Scott & Knight, February.

Tri-ang Minic No. M228 Double Decker Bus, in 1950s Hull livery with Push-N-Go Motor, light wear to the destination panel above the rear entrance, otherwise excellent plus. Comes in scarce box. Sold for £120, Vectis, February.

LEGO No. 6285 Pirate Ship, in original box. Sold for £85, East Bristol Auctions, January.

LEGO Eldorado Fortress No. 6276, in original box. Sold for £60, East Bristol Auctions, January.

Scalextric C11 Competition Super Electra, in the original Grand Prix flag window box with instructions, very good condition, box fair to good. Sold for £35, Lacy, Scott & Knight, February.

Palitoy Action Man Scorpion Tank, in original box. Sold for £48, East Bristol Auctions, January.

Palitoy Action Man Jeep, in original box, complete with folding windscreen and flag. Sold for £42, East Bristol Auctions, January.

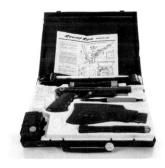

Topper Toys Secret Sam Agent's Case, including pistol, periscope, silencer, rifle stock, camera, message missile, four bullets and instructions. Very good, lacks two bullets. Sold for £90, Special Auction Services, March.

Minic Motorways No. 1531 International Circuit Extension Set, in the original box, includes racing pit, automatic starting gate, flags, fencing etc. Transfers applied and has been used. Sold for £40, Lacy, Scott & Knight, February.

Lone Star Roll Ticket Machine, toy bus conductor's ticket machine, some spare rolls of tickets, lapel badge and carrying strap. Good plus in fair to good card box. Sold for £25, Vectis, February.

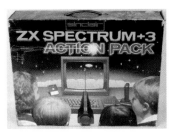

Sinclair ZX Spectrum +3 Action Pack, including Sinclair ZX Spectrum, light gun, joystick, instruction manual, power unit and six games, in the original box with all internal packaging. Sold for £55, Lacy, Scott & Knight, February.

Schuco No. 4000 Girato Mercedes 250SE, opening doors and steerable front wheels and plated parts, motor in working order with correct Schuco key. Sold for £50, Vectis, February.

Tri-ang Scalextric K703 Control Tower Kit, unmade, with instructions, in original box, very good, contents not checked. Sold for £200, Special Auction Services, March.

Tri-ang Electric Powered RMS Orcades Ocean Liner, with plastic constructed body, house in the original box. Sold for £40, Biddle & Webb, March.

Palitoy Action Man Soldier Bivouac, item has never been removed from the card, large tear to cellophane, condition is near mint on a good card. Sold for £520, Vectis, May.

Japanese The Abominable Snowman, fur covering, a few patches missing, some soiling. Replaced remote control. Sold for $200, Morphy Auctions, May.

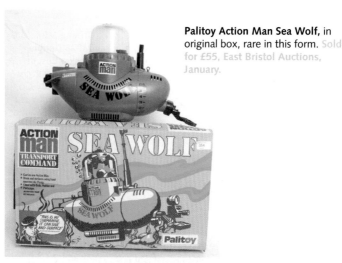

Palitoy Action Man Sea Wolf, in original box, rare in this form. Sold for £55, East Bristol Auctions, January.

Century 21 Toys Battery Operated Moon Bus, lacks one rubber track but does have 'Sword Captain' badge in box, otherwise good plus in a fair illustrated box. Sold for £35, Vectis, February.

Telex (UK) Model Assembly Kit, scare 1950s British kit featuring plastic bodies for motor coach, saloon car, racing car and lorry. Excellent in a good plus illustrated box. Sold for £45, Vectis, February.

Scalextric C76 Mini Cooper, condition generally good plus with maintenance instruction leaflet and good hinged lid box (missing inner packing). Sold for £25, Vectis, June.

Palitoy Action Man Soldier Mine Detection Set No. 34117, item has never been removed from the card. The card is complete with one tear at the top. Condition is mint on good plus card. Sold for £280, Vectis, May.

Scalextric C56 Lister Jaguar, condition generally good plus with fair lift off lid box and inner packing. Sold for £30, Vectis, June.

Palitoy Action Man Soldier Helmet and Small Arms Set No. 93735640, item has never been removed from the card, condition is mint on an excellent card. Sold for £220, Vectis, May.

Palitoy Action Man Soldier Flame Thrower Set No. 93735690, item has never been removed from the card, condition is mint on an excellent card. Sold for £120, Vectis, May.

Subbuteo Fivesides, contents complete, condition is generally excellent to mint in an excellent lift off lid box. Sold for £45, Vectis, June.

Palitoy Action Man Soldier Bunk Bed Set No. 34221, item has never been removed from the card, condition is mint on an excellent card. Sold for £80, Vectis, May.

Jetex Jet Propelled Racing Car, various accessories and fuel pellets, good to excellent for display, in a fair to good illustrated box. Sold for £40, Vectis, July.

Palitoy Action Man Pilot Scramble Set No. 94037500, item has never been removed from the card, condition is mint on an excellent card. Sold for £240, Vectis, May.

Palitoy Action Man Soldier Field Radio and Telephone Set No. 93735600, item has never been removed from the card, the cellophane has a small tear. Condition is mint on a good plus card. Sold for £260, Vectis, May.

Raphael Lipkin No. 1115 Pippin Toys Massey Ferguson 780 Combine Harvester, would benefit from a light clean, some paint loss to driver otherwise overall excellent with a fair, sun faded box. Sold for £220, Vectis, July.

Palitoy Action Man Explorer Base Camp Set No. 94035004, item has never been removed from the card, there is one split at the bottom, condition is near mint on a good card. Sold for £600, Vectis, May.

Laurie Toys Tow-away Glider Set Rolls-Royce, hairline crack to roof, overall good plus to excellent for display, with good plus box. Sold for £60, Vectis, July.

Clifford Series Ford Cortina with Trailer, would benefit from a light clean, near mint in good box. Sold for £60, Vectis, July.

Palitoy Action Man Pilot Crash Helmet Set No. 94037510, item has never been removed from the card, condition is mint on an excellent card. Sold for £340, Vectis, May.

Telsada No. 25004 Vauxhall Victor 101 Estate Car, mark to roof, missing spare wheel and friction driver does not work. Sold for £45, Vectis, July.

Phix (Hong Kong) remote control Space Capsule, circa 1966, missing battery box, some plating loss to rear of model, fair with a fair card box. Sold for £15, Vectis, July.

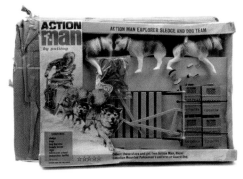

Palitoy Action Man Explorer Sledge and Dog Team No. 35002, item has never been removed from the card, shrink wrap cellophane pulled too tight causing distortion and one very small tear. Condition is mint on an excellent card. Sold for £480, Vectis, May.

Palitoy Action Man Explorer Sleeping Bag Set No. 94035203, the item has never been removed from the card, condition is mint on an excellent card. Sold for £130, Vectis, May.

ebuys

We round up some of the best collecting highlights sold throughout the year on eBay.

Ebay, no matter what way you look at it has revolutionised the collecting market - some would say for the best, while others may think it's actually been for the worst. However, there's certainly no disputing that eBay does throw up some fantastic collectables that you might not find anywhere else.

Back when it was launched in 1995 it must have seemed like a curious website that might occasionally have some interesting items for sale but since then it has grown into one of the biggest websites in the world with a turnover of millions. Of course, back in those early days you could use the website to pick up a bargain because not many people used it and sellers weren't always aware of an item's value. However, now there are millions of collectors around the wolrd who ensure the price on eBay is often pushed up well above what the same toy may have sold for at a traditional auction or toy fair - as you will probably see from the items listed here.

eBay can also be a useful tool when you're checking to see how much your toys might be worth, as you can quickly search for similar pieces listed on the website. However, don't fall into the trap of looking at a 'Buy it Now' price for a current listing and thinking your toy is worth the same. The best thing to do is tick the 'sold listings' box when searching so you'll get a clearer picture of what items sold and how much they actually sold for. Although even then, make sure the item in question wasn't re-listed at a later date if the original sale fell through. ■

⬆ Crescent Toys Dan Dare figures, an "exceptional set" according to the seller, who also noted the last example he saw sold for more than £2,000. This piece was in unplayed condition. **Sold for £1,600 (19 bids).**

⬆ Denys Fisher Stretch Armstrong, remember this? Have fun stretching and bending Armstrong until his limbs inevitably snap off. The figure was in excellent order, according to the listing. **Sold for £450 (one bid).**

⬆ Heusser Hela Bobsleigh with Elastolin figures, dashing through the snow comes this scarce 18cm long sleigh. Made around 1930 there was some wear to the figures. **Sold for £725 (Buy it Now).**

⬆ Britains Fordson Major Tractor & Rear Dump Trailer set, dating from 1964, the model was in very good condition with some paint loss, while the trailer had some repairs and repro decals. **Sold for £510 (16 bids).**

⬆ Tri-ang Minic No. 50ME Rolls Royce Sedanca Electric, the model was in excellent condition and also came with its original instruction leaflet and key, plus a very good box. **Sold for £461 (27 bids).**

⬆ Dinky Toys No. 514 Weetabix Guy Van, have you had your Weetabix? If not then this nice example of the Dinky model would have certainly been the thing for you. Re-listed due to non-payment. **Sold for £623 (30 bids).**

DIECAST | RAILWAYS | TOY FIGURES | TINPLATE | TV & FILM | OTHERS | EBUYS

↟ **Corgi Toys No. 497 Man from UNCLE Gun Firing Thrush-Buster,** this was the rare USA issue finished in cream. The model and box were both listed as being in near mint condition. **Sold for £679 (Buy it Now).**

↟ **Pre-production Mini-Dinky No. 17 Aston Martin DB6,** eBay throws up some interesting lots, like this rare test example from 1967/68 for the planned Mini-Dinky range. **Sold for £717 (31 bids).**

↟ **Corgi Toys Spider-Man Gift Set,** do whatever a spider can with this superb example of the brightly-coloured Spider-Man Gift Set. The bike also featured the rare white wheels. **Sold for £659.99 (Buy it Now).**

↟ **Dinky Toys No. 505 Foden Flat Truck with Chains,** this was the first type of the fabulous Foden, which was a "very near perfect example" according to the listing. **Sold for £1,550 (three bids).**

↟ **Dinky Toys No. 39e Chrysler Royal Sedan,** normally 'very rare' in a listing sounds some alarm bells but clearly this piece was considered to be scarce as it sold for just under the price guide of £800 to £1,100. **Sold for £745 (Buy it Now).**

↟ **Mattel Masters of the Universe He-Man and Battle Cat,** another "ultra rare" listing, this 1980s action figure was inspired by the famous television series and featured He-Man along with his heroic steed. **Sold for £455 (22 bids).**

↟ **LEGO System Set No. 810,** you can see how LEGO has come a long way from this vintage set, which was "virtually unplayed with". **Sold for £446 (39 bids).**

↟ **Scalextric Aston Martin DB4,** this was part of a collection that had come from the seller's uncle. It ran well and the lights were also in working condition. **Sold for £430.19 (24 bids).**

↟ **Louis Marx Batman Hot-Line Batphone,** at the first sign of trouble the Batphone flashes red. No jokers were bidding on this but, riddle me this... how much did it sell for? **Sold for £379 (17 bids).**

↟ **Denys Fisher Doctor Who Leela,** although the box had some slight damage the figure had only been removed once for the sake of the eBay listing. **Sold for £361 (five bids).**

↟ **Make Your Own Dan Dare Space-ship,** manufactured by Wallis Rigby in 1954, this book allowed the owner to press out a series of space-ship parts to build their own rocket. **Sold for £360 (two bids).**

↟ **Tippco Volkswagen Coca Cola Truck,** although based on the all-American fizzy drink, this truck was actually made in Germany around 1954. The box, however, was a repro. **Sold for £320 (Buy it Now).**

↟ **Telsalda Morris Mini Cooper,** hailing from the 1960s this plastic friction drive vehicle came in its original picture box and measured five inches long. A fine item for a Mini fan. **Sold for £114.88 (13 bids).**

↟ **French Dinky Toys 24V Buick Roadmaster,** this was the second issue type with cross hatch inside roof - considered rare by the seller. In very near mint condition. **Sold for £670 (28 bids).**

↟ **Matchbox Superfast MB70 Ferrari 308,** this was the bright red pre-production version, which also came with a white interior and without a part number to the base. **Sold for £617 (30 bids).**

↟ **The Avengers Jigsaw Puzzles,** made in the 1960s and believed to be exclusive to Woolworth's, this vendor was selling four complete *Avengers* puzzles. Each had 340 pieces. **Sold for £599 (one bid).**

↟ **Matchbox Superfast MB4 '57 Chevy,** another pre-production Matchbox from the same seller as our previous Matchbox choice (rockertrontoys). Again it was in great condition. **Sold for £822 (36 bids).**

↟ **Heroquest Wizards of Morcar expansion,** some old Games Workshop board games are becoming exceptionally collectable and therefore valuable. **Sold for £510 (28 bids).**

↟ **Dinky Supertoys No. 908 Mighty Antar Transformer,** "a superb example of a very hard to find desirable commercial" read the description and we're inclined to agree. A cracking piece. **Sold for £950 (Buy it Now).**

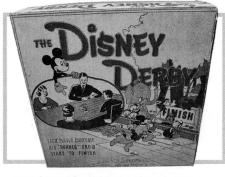

↟ **Metal-Wood Repititions Co. The Disney Derby,** created by a Sydney-based company, the game allowed players to race famous Disney characters like Mickey Mouse and Donald Duck. **Sold for £845 (24 bids).**

↟ **Nomura Battery Operated Batman,** easily one of the best Batman collectables out there. This large tinplate robot was made in Japan and came with its original, charming illustrated box. **Sold for £2,326 (29 bids).**

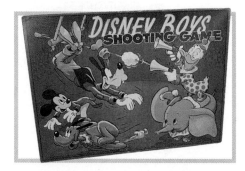

↟ **Chad Valley Disney Boys Shooting Game,** not a game for your little sister according to the box. Poor old Mickey and the gang were forced to be the victims of your target practice. In good condition, some wear. **Sold for £445 (four bids).**

↟ **Dinky Toys Gift Set No. 4 Racing Cars,** made between 1953 and 1954 this was a rare set, claimed the seller. Most of the cars had the "odd nick/scuff" while the HWM suffered a few more. **Sold for £425 (19 bids).**

↟ **Ichimura Batman Jeep,** here's one of the more unusual Batman collectables. Made in Japan in conjunction with the 1966 live action TV series, the Jeep featured some bright illustrations of the Dynamic Duo in action. **Sold for £920 (four bids).**

⬧ Scalextric c70 Bugatti, to emphasise the rarity of this piece, the vendor noted that only 20 to 40 are believed to still be around today, saying it was the ultimate collectable Scalextric car. Sold for £5,465 (29 bids).

⬧ Denys Fisher Stretch Hulk, "you won't like me when I'm stretchy" was the famous phrase! In perfect condition, which is unusual as they tend to leak with age, this was Incredible. Sold for £1,399 (Buy it Now).

⬧ Dinky Toys 28 Series Kodak Van, dating back to 1935 it's amusing to think of this now being sold on a hi-tech site like eBay - who would have guess all those years ago?! Sold for £1,019 (33 bids).

⬧ Corgi Toys No. 267 Batmobile, the iconic toy of the iconic car. An excellent near mint model in an excellent box with all the flaps intact and complete with instructions. Sold for £1,294 (Buy it Now).

⬧ Matchbox No. 66 Yellow Citroen DS 16, normally descriptions go into great detail but clearly this particular seller must have thought the model spoke for itself, as he only noted 'boxed'. Sold for £706 (35 bids).

⬧ Rabbit Tin Toy Scooter, a charming tinplate scooter from a Japanese maker called Rabbit. Bought in the '60s, it had been kept in storage ever since and, as such, was in almost ex shop stock condition. Sold for £1,005 (17 bids).

⬧ Corgi Toys Gift Set 21 Chipperfields Circus, made from 1969 until 1971 this was a cracking set for a diecast collector, particularly as the seller rated the condition as 9.5+/10. Sold for £951 (27 bids).

⬧ Noddy Woo Woo Locomotive, the seller had never seen a complete example of this set from the 1960s, which included a nodding Noddy figure driving a train. It was in good condition. Sold for £665 (two bids).

⬧ Plaston Mike Mercury's Supercar, measuring an impressive 12-inches, this was a brilliant toy for a Gerry Anderson fan and even the box had some great artwork of the famous flying car. Sold for £890 (33 bids).

⬧ Meccano No. 2 Constructor Car Garage, measuring an impressive 14.25-inches, this would be the perfect place to store your prized model motor. Dating from the 1930s, it was in "super, original condition". Sold for £775 (Buy it Now).

⬧ Corgi Toys No. 349 Morris Mini Mostest Pop Art Box Only, that's right, this listing didn't even include the model... just the box for this sought after piece. Sold for £700 (58 bids).

⬧ Foden Shackleton Tipper Truck, in excellent condition the truck had a few small marks but came with its key, spanner and tipper mechanism lever. Box suffered from wear over a period of 60 plus years. Sold for £575 (Buy it Now).

↟ Britains No. 171F Fordson Power Major Metal Wheeled Tractor, a very nice example of this brightly-coloured blue and red tractor with some slight shelf wear to the box. Ex shop stock. **Sold for £970 (13 bids).**

↟ Corgi Toys GS21 Chipperfields Circus Crane, Scammell Cab & Menagerie Trailer Set, 100% complete and 100% original boasted the listing for this very clean example. **Sold for £699.95 (Buy it Now).**

↟ Corgi Toys GS40 The Avengers, another very nice Corgi Gift Set, this time inspired by the adventures of Steed and Emma Peel. In superb condition, complete with three original umbrellas. **Sold for £601 (11 bids).**

↟ Tri-ang Scalextric Super 124 Lotus Indianapolis Ref 24C-500 Ace GP, finished in 1/24 scale this delightful slot car had decals in pretty good condition and 'ok' tyres. **Sold for £575 (three bids).**

↟ Codeg Mechanical Dalek, these tinplate Daleks from Codeg are among the most sought after *Doctor Who* collectables. This example was in excellent working condition, with some faults. **Sold for £489 (Buy it Now).**

↟ Lehmann No. 683 Halloh Motorcyclist, here's a bit of a 'fixer upper' because the motor didn't work on this vintage wind-up toy. Still, that didn't deter everyone and several bidders fancied a project. **Sold for £1,030 (32 bids).**

↟ Crescent Toys Atomic Jet Gun, no, don't worry, this doesn't shoot deadly rays of radiation, instead it's a water pistol based on the 'Hiller' Atom Ray Gun from the 1940s. The box had some wear. **Sold for £500 (one bid).**

↟ Clifford Series F1 Car Transporter, similar to the superb Corgi Ecurie Ecosse transporter, this equally impressive plastic version hailed from the 1950s and came with three plastic cars. **Sold for £490 (24 bids).**

↟ Multiple Toy Makers Steve Zodiac's Fireball XL5 Space City Playset, made in 1964, it's rare to see this impressive large-scale toy in such amazing condition, let alone with the box. **Sold for £1,435 (Best Offer).**

↟ Lesney Moko Prime Mover Trailer and Bulldozer, this example was complete with the "elusive loading ramps and tow piece" according to the description. The trailer and ramp did both have some paint loss. **Sold for £1,021 (35 bids).**

↟ Tri-ang Spot-On No. 109/2P ERF 68g with Wood Plank Load, rated a modest 9.5/10 by the seller, this was the scarce golden yellow version. The box was also rated 9.5/10 and came with the inner packing. **Sold for £825.09 (17 bids).**

↟ Lesney Matchbox Toys No. MB56a Trolley Bus 'Visco-Static', both the model and the box on this bright red replica were original and in near mint condition, according to the eBay listing. **Sold for £822 (38 bids).**

↟ **Marx Toys Fred Flintstones Flivver,**
measuring 20cm this 'Flivver', which means a car that gives a rough ride in case you're interested, is certainly unusual. Dating from the 1960s. **Sold for £525 (Buy it Now).**

↟ **Golden Gate Fireball XL5 Steve Zodiac and Zonnie Jetmobile,** circa 1961, the condition of this rare Gerry Anderson toy was good after being kept in a shoebox in the loft for 53 years. **Listed at £1,275 (Best Offer accepted).**

↟ **Hasbro Transformers G1 Autobot Warrior Tracks,** Transformers toys certainly seem to be going well at the moment, with prices often soaring into four figures. This example was still sealed and was described as near mint. **£1,550 (25 bids).**

↟ **Scalextric 007 James Bond Boxed Set,**
despite missing a few items, including a front headlight on the Bandit car, this classic Scalextric set still caught the attention of the bidders. **Sold for £1,000 (13 bids).**

↟ **Dinky Toys No. 23a Pre-War 'Humbug',**
the seller was clearly loathe to sell this rare piece to fund a new 'project'. It was listed as being in exceptional condition. **Sold for £875 (nine bids).**

↟ **Hot Wheels Rrrumblers Gift Set,** here's a very rare set for all you Hot Wheels fans, featuring six brightly coloured motorcycles, including the Bone Shaker and Praying Mantis. **Sold for £702 (31 bids).**

↟ **Tri-ang Spot-On No. 211 Austin Seven,**
decent diecast seems to perform well on eBay, as this Austin Seven shows. Condition was clean, some tiny areas of chipped paint and a slightly loose end flap on the box. **Sold for £698 (33 bids).**

↟ **Corgi Toys No. 270 James Bond Aston Martin DB5,** this was the original from 1968, complete with a mint box/display plinth. Mint condition, with ther seller saying he had never seen such a pristine one. **Sold for £655 (21 bids).**

↟ **Subbuteo Ultra Journey into Space Set,**
here's something unusual from Subbuteo, normally associated with sports games. From 1957, it was a space race game from Subbuteo creator Peter Adolph. **Listed at £1,800 (Best Offer accepted)**

↟ **Tri-ang Minic No. 30M Mechanical Horse & Pantechnicon 'Brockhouse',** produced in 1951 this tinplate clockwork replica was still in full working order and with its original key. **Sold for £1,750 (Buy it Now).**

↟ **Corgi Toys Gift Set 16 Ecurie Ecosse Transporter,** an opportunity to pick-up this delightful Gift Set. The vehicles and box were in very good condition. A very attractive piece! **Sold for £299.99 (Buy it Now)**

↟ **Lesney Matchbox Toys MB51c 8-Wheel Tipper 'Alcan on the Move',** a rare promo from Matchbox, complete with its original box. The model was in near mint condition, with a minor mark to the windscreen. **Sold for £705 (42 bids).**

↟ **Corgi GS38 Rallye Monte Carlo Gift Set,** certainly one of the prettiest Corgi gift sets out there, this attracted a lot of attention on eBay. "Superb!" exclaimed the seller and we're inclined to agree. **Sold for £1,999 (Buy it Now).**

↟ **Spot-On No. 110/3D AEC Mammoth Major Flat Float with Sides and Oil Drums,** "a great opportunity to collect a very rare item, I think it's near impossible to find a better one," explained the seller. **Sold for £1,421 (36 bids).**

↟ **Mego Batman and Robin Magnetic Fly-Away Action figures,** the Dynamic Duo never looked better. In fact they were still attached to their original card inserts and had been in storage for 15 years. **Sold for £1,250 (Buy it Now).**

↟ **Lesney Matchbox 1-75 Series No. 22c Red Pontiac GP Coupe,** it was actually the box (a very rare Type F example) that was the main selling point for this red model, the seller notes it's not a reproduction. **Sold for £919 (12 bids).**

↟ **Louis Marx Dalek Construction Kit,** normally more likely to be destructive than constructive, this plastic Dalek kit was certainly a stunning item. Incredibly it had never been built. **Sold for £771 (12 bids).**

↟ **Dinky Toys No. 901 Foden Diesel Eight Wheel Wagon,** just like your more typical auctions, Dinky trucks always do well online and so did this example, despite some general wear. **Sold for £825 (Buy it Now).**

↟ **Dinky Toys Pre-War Kodak Delivery Van,** "what you see is what you get" is often a phrase seen on eBay and it was attributed to this slightly battered Delivery Van, which had some wear/tear and a broken back axle. **Sold for £600 (one bid).**

↟ **Lesney Moko Muffin the Mule,** his Muffin the Mule is one of the earlier Lesney toys. Often tricky to find with all the strings intact, this was meant to be in excellent condition. **Sold for £560 (22 bids).**

↟ **Dinky Toys No. 505 Foden Flat Truck with Chains,** the "rarest post-War Dinky" read the listing for this truck, as according to the seller only a few were produced in maroon. Condition was described as excellent. **Sold for £1,500 (one bid).**

↟ **Dinky Toys Gift Set 149 Competition Sports Cars,** rated 9.5/10 by the seller, the box had been repaired. Still that didn't put off the bidders who quickly pushed up the price. **Sold for £1,085 (32 bids).**

↟ **Dinky Toys No. 514 Guy Van 'Weetabix',** one of the rarer Dinky vans due to its short production run, the model had been given the odd paint touch up and had some paint bubbles on the roof. **Sold for £747 (31 bids).**

↟ **Tri-ang Minic Pre-War Clockwork No. 39M Taxi Cab,** this rare colour variation was made in the 1930s and is now very hard to find, according to the seller. Complete with working motor. **Sold for £585 (Buy it Now).**